THE
MOTHERLAND
CALLS

THE MOTHERLAND CALLS

STEPHEN BOURNE

BRITAIN'S BLACK
SERVICEMEN
& WOMEN
1939–45

The
History
Press

Front cover: Pilot Officer Peter Thomas. *Courtesy of the Imperial War Museum*
Back cover: Nadia Cattouse. *Courtesy of Nadia Cattouse*

First published 2012

The History Press
The Mill, Brimscombe Port
Stroud, Gloucestershire, GL5 2QG
www.thehistorypress.co.uk

British Library Cataloguing in Publication Data.
A catalogue record for this book is available from the British Library.

ISBN 978 0 7524 6585 2

Typesetting and origination by The History Press
Printed in Great Britain

CONTENTS

ACKNOWLEDGEMENTS

Black and Asian Studies Association
BBC Written Archives Centre
British Film Institute (www.bfi.org.uk)
British Library (www.bl.uk)
Commonwealth War Graves Commission (www.cwgc.org)
Imperial War Museum (London) (www.iwm.org.uk)
London Borough of Southwark Libraries
West Indian Ex-Services Association
www.caribbeanaircrew-ww2.com
Nadia Cattouse
Sean Creighton
Neil Flanigan MBE (President, West Indian Ex-Services Association)
Steven Hatton (Director, *Into the Wind*)
Keith Howes
Linda Bourne Hull
Deborah Joyce
Professor David Killingray
Sam King MBE
Barnaby Phillips (Director, *The Burma Boy*)
Laurent Phillpot (Archivist, West Indian Ex-Services Association)
Francesca Pratt (Stock Services, Southwark Libraries)
Marika Sherwood (Senior Researcher, Institute of Commonwealth Studies)
Aaron Smith
Robert Taylor
Patrick Vernon (Director, *Speaking Out & Standing Firm* and *A Charmed Life*)

AUTHOR'S NOTE

In *The Motherland Calls* the terms 'black' and 'African-Caribbean' refer to Caribbean and British people of African origin. Other terms, such as 'West Indian', 'negro' and 'coloured' are used in their historical contexts, usually before the 1960s and 1970s, the decades in which the term 'black' came into popular use.

This book's purpose is as an introduction to the subject; it is not intended to be definitive; the reader will find gaps.

For information about the Home Front the reader should consult my previous book, *Mother Country: Britain's Black Community on the Home Front, 1939–45* (The History Press, 2010).

The Motherland Calls should not be read in isolation. Since the 1980s several books have been published about the lives of black servicemen and women in the Second World War. Some of these are now out of print, but I would suggest that readers access them through interlibrary loans, the British Library, or a second-hand book dealer, such as www.abebooks.co.uk. I would highly recommend the following: Ben Bousquet and Colin Douglas's *West Indian Women at War: British Racism in World War II* (1991); Oliver Marshall's *The Caribbean at War: British West Indians in World War II* (1992); and Robert N. Murray's *Lest We Forget: The Experiences of World War II West Indian Ex-Service Personnel* (1996). Angelina Osborne and Arthur Torrington's *We Served: The Untold Story of the West Indian Contribution to World War II* (2005) and Eric Myers-Davis's *Under One Flag: How indigenous and ethnic peoples of the Commonwealth and British Empire helped Great Britain win World War II* (2009), aimed at younger readers, are extremely useful and beautifully produced.

Autobiographies or memoirs written by black ex-servicemen and women are harder to find, but the exceptions include: E. Martin Noble's *Jamaica Airman: A Black Airman in Britain 1943 and After* (1984); Lilian Bader's *Together: Lilian Bader: Wartime Memoirs of a WAAF 1939–1944* (1989); Dudley Thompson's *From Kingston to Kenya: The Making of a Pan-Africanist Lawyer* (1993); Sam King's *Climbing Up the Rough Side of the Mountain* (1998); Isaac Fadoyebo's *A Stroke of Unbelievable Luck* (1999); and Cy Grant's *'A Member of the RAF of Indeterminate Race': WW2 experiences of a former RAF navigator and POW* (2006).

The experiences of African American GIs in Britain from 1942–45 have been extensively covered by Graham Smith in *When Jim Crow Met John Bull: Black American Soldiers in World War II Britain* (1987). For West Indians and others, readers may want to consult the works of Marika Sherwood, including her book *Many Struggles: West Indian Workers and Service Personnel in Britain (1939–1945)* (1985); as well as back issues of the newsletters of the Black and Asian Studies Association, co-founded in 1991 by Marika Sherwood, Stephen Bourne and several other historians of black Britain. The experiences of Africans in wartime have been covered extensively by Professor David Killingray in several books, including his comprehensive *Fighting for Britain: African Soldiers in the Second World War* (2010). See also Roger Lambo's excellent chapter, 'Achtung! The Black Prince: West Africans in the Royal Air Force 1939–46' in *Africans in Britain* (1994), edited by Professor David Killingray.

Joanne Buggins's 'West Indians in Britain during the Second World War: a short history drawing on Colonial Office papers', published in the *Imperial War Museum Review No. 5* (1990), is highly recommended.

The following website is an invaluable source of information on Caribbean aircrew in the Second World War: www.caribbeanaircrew-ww2.com.

Several exhibitions have made important contributions to documenting the experiences of black servicemen and women, and these include 'Butetown Remembers World War II: Seamen, the Forces, Evacuees' at the Butetown History and Arts Centre, Cardiff Bay (15 March – 3 July 2005) and 'From War to Windrush' at the Imperial War Museum, London (13 June 2008 – 29 March 2009) (see Appendix II). The Royal Air Force Museum in London (www.rafmuseum.org.uk) has a permanent exhibition on display that acknowledges ethnic diversity in the RAF in the Second World War.

Though every care has been taken, if, through inadvertence or failure to trace the present owners, I have included any copyright material without acknowledgement or permission, I offer my apologies to all concerned.

STATISTICS

Exact statistics of the number of black men and women from Britain, the Caribbean and Africa who served in the British armed services during the Second World War, or contributed to the war effort, are impossible to determine. Ethnicity was not automatically recorded and no official records of all those working in the many fields of production for the war effort were kept.

Juliet Gardiner, author of *Wartime Britain 1939–1945* (2004), claims that on the day war broke out, 3 September 1939, there were no more than 8,000 black people living in Britain. However, some historians of black Britain have suggested a much higher figure, including Dr Hakim Adi (around 15,000).[1] The recruitment of black people from the colonies into the war effort changed this situation but, without official figures, estimates vary.

In 1995, using a variety of Colonial Office sources, Ian Spencer estimated in his contribution to *War Culture* that, of British Caribbeans in military service during the war, 10,270 were from Jamaica, 800 from Trinidad, 417 from British Guiana, and a smaller number, not exceeding 1,000, came from other Caribbean colonies. The majority served in the RAF.[2]

In *We Were There*, published in 2002 by the Ministry of Defence, it is claimed:

At the end of the war over three million men [from various parts of the British Empire] were under arms, 2.5 million of them in the Indian Army, over 200,000 from East Africa and 150,000 from West Africa. The RAF also recruited personnel from across the Commonwealth. At first, recruitment concentrated on British subjects of European descent. However, after October 1939 questions of nationality and race were put aside, and all Commonwealth people became eligible to join the RAF on equal terms. By the end of the war over 17,500 such men and women had volunteered to join the RAF, in a variety of roles, and a further 25,000 served in the Royal Indian Air Force.[3]

In 2007 Richard Smith noted in *The Oxford Companion to Black British History*:

From 1941 the British government began to recruit service personnel and skilled workers in the West Indies for service in the United Kingdom. Over 12,000 saw active service in the Royal Air Force ... About 600 West Indian women were recruited for the Auxiliary Territorial Service, arriving in Britain in the autumn of 1943. The enlistment of these volunteers was accomplished despite official misgivings and obstruction.[4]

In 1995 the Imperial War Museum produced 'Together', a multimedia resource pack on the contribution made in the Second World War by African, Asian and Caribbean men and women. In the pack's introduction it is noted that there are no exact statistics for the number of men and women of African, Caribbean and Asian origin who served in the British forces during the war, but it does offer the most accurate information that could be found at that time on the numbers of black wartime personnel.

WEST INDIES

Several thousand West Indians were recruited into the British war effort. Nearly 6,000 served with the RAF, 5,536 as ground staff and 300 as aircrew. Thousands more served in the merchant navy and in civilian war work in Britain, 350 of them in munitions. Approximately 700 British Hondurans came and worked as lumberjacks in Scotland. In addition, 40,000 West Indians were recruited for work in the USA.

Early in 1940, 1,800 responded to a Colonial Office request for merchant seamen. In 1942 there was a call for skilled engineers. In the army there had been a colour bar, but it was relaxed for the war and some West Indians joined the Royal Engineers in 1941. There were, however, disagreements between the Colonial Office, who favoured recruiting West Indians, and the Secretary of State for War, who was reluctant. In 1944 a Caribbean Regiment was raised, comprising 1,000 soldiers, and after training they were sent overseas but never actually saw active service.

The most significant contribution was in the RAF. Some West Indians trained with the Royal Canadian Air Force (RCAF) before coming to Britain. Between 1940 and 1942, 3,000 enlisted in the RAF and between June and November 1944, nearly 4,000 ground staff arrived in Britain. A further 1,500 came over in March 1945. Of those serving in the RAF and RCAF, 103 were decorated.

On a smaller scale, women also played a part. The reluctance of the War Office to recruit women from the West Indies explains the relatively small number, but 80 joined the Women's Auxiliary Air Force (WAAF) and 30 the Auxiliary Territorial Service (ATS).[5]

AFRICA

The total number of Africans who fought for Britain in the Second World War is approximately 372,000: 119,000 were under South-East Asia Command (SEAC) – 46,000 East Africans and 73,000 West Africans; 47,500 Africans served in the Middle East – 31,000 of them East Africans and 16,500 of them West Africans; a further 206,000 served in the Home Commands in Africa – 150,000 of them East Africans and 56,000 of them West Africans.

The two main forces fighting for Britain were the King's African Rifles (KAR) and the Royal West African Frontier Force (RWAFF, known as Waff). A large number of KAR battalions, raised from Uganda, Kenya, Tanganyika, Nyasaland and Somaliland, took part in three major campaigns of the war: the defeat of the Italians in Somaliland and Abyssinia, 1940–41; the occupation of Madagascar against the Vichy French in 1942; and the re-conquest of Burma against the Japanese in 1944 and 1945. It was the first time that KAR battalions had fought outside the continent of Africa. Originally deployed to fight the Italians in East Africa, the askaris (local troops) of the KAR were available for other battlefronts after the defeat of the Italians. The entry of Japan into the war made it necessary to recruit larger forces to fight them in the Far East. By May 1942 there were 28 battalions operating overseas. Over 12,000 members of the 11th East African Division were front-line troops in the Burma Campaign. The sickness rate of East African troops was lower than that of other contingents and they adapted well to the wide variety of climates and terrains that faced them.

In addition, 10,000 Bechuana (from what is now Botswana) volunteered for service with the British Army and served in Syria, Egypt, Sicily, Italy and the Middle East. Forty-five of them were given honours or awards.

The RWAFF also played an important part in the Second World War, firstly in the Abyssinian Campaign of 1941, and later in the Burma Campaign of 1943–44. 81 West African Division consisted of three brigades: one from Nigeria, one from the Gold Coast and one from Sierra Leone. They were trained in jungle warfare before being sent to India in September 1943 and thence to Burma. In 1944 a further division of West African troops was formed, the 82 (WA) Division, and these operated with the Indian XV Corps during the next campaign in Arakan, Burma. The West African troops in Burma were renowned for their discipline and there were awards for bravery and gallantry: one soldier was given the British Empire Medal (BEM), three the Distinguished Conduct Medal (DCM), eleven the Military Medal (MM) and seventeen were Mentioned in Despatches.[6]

Notes

1 See Stephen Bourne, *Mother Country: Britain's Black Community on the Home Front, 1939–45* (The History Press, 2010), p. 135.

2   Ian Spencer, 'World War Two and the Making of Multi-Racial Britain', in *War Culture: Social Change and Changing Experience in World War Two*, ed. Pat Kirkham and David Thoms (Lawrence and Wishart, 1995), p. 212.

3   *We Were There: For 200 years ethnic minorities have fought for Britain all over the world* (Director General Corporate Communications/Ministry of Defence, 2002), p. 13.

4   Richard Smith, 'Second World War', *The Oxford Companion to Black British History* (Oxford University Press, 2007), pp. 436–7.

5   Imperial War Museum, 'Together'.

6   Ibid.

INTRODUCTION

'We did a damn good job and when Winston Churchill said "Never was so much owed by so many to so few" I'm proud to say I am one of the few.'
Baron Baker (RAF) in *The Invisible Force* (BBC Radio 4, 16 May 1989)

In 2002, when the bestselling author Ken Follett published his wartime espionage thriller *Hornet Flight*, he wasn't expecting criticism for including a black Royal Air Force (RAF) squadron leader in his novel. The squadron leader, Charles Ford, is featured in the prologue with a Caribbean accent 'overlaid with an Oxbridge drawl'.[1] One of Follett's severest critics was Alan Frampton, who served as a pilot in the RAF between 1942 and 1946. Writing to Follett from his home in Zimbabwe, Frampton said Ford was 'not a credible character' and that his inclusion was a 'sop' to black people who may read *Hornet Flight*. An angry Frampton apparently threw down the book in disgust when he came across the Ford character.

In his letter to Follett, Frampton said:

For the life of me I cannot recall ever encountering a black airman of any rank whatsoever during the whole of my service, which included Bomber Command. This may have been a coincidence of course but, in England sixty years ago, blacks were few and far between amongst the population and race was not an issue, unlike today with its attendant racial tensions and extreme sensitivity amounting almost to paranoia. He certainly aroused my indignation, remembering as I do, the real heroes of that period in our history, who were not black. I regard myself as a realist but certainly not an apologist for my race. I have read several of your books and enjoyed them. This one I threw down in disgust.

In his reply to Frampton, dated 19 November 2003, Ken Follett explained:

I'm afraid you're mistaken. The character Charles was inspired by the father of a friend of mine, a Trinidadian who flew eighty sorties as a navigator in the Second World War and reached the rank of squadron leader. He says there were 252 Trinidadians in the RAF, most of them officers. He was the highest ranked during the war, although after the war a few reached wing commander.

He received the DFC and the DSO. With true-life heroes as he, there's no need for a 'sop' to black people, really, is there?

The Trinidadian who inspired Follett is Ulric Cross (see Chapter 8) whose response to Frampton was also put on record: 'He must be living in a strange world. I am old enough to have a certain amount of tolerance. People believe what they need to believe. For some reason Frampton needs to believe that. When you know what you have done, what people think is irrelevant.'[2]

Some may view Alan Frampton's outburst as racist, but it should be taken into account that, with the erasure of black servicemen and women from the history books, Frampton probably had no way of knowing that black RAF officers, like Ulric Cross, existed. After 1945 historians of the Second World War, as well as the media, portrayed the conflict as one that only involved white servicemen and women. Regrettably, this has continued to be the case, even after the West Indian Ex-Servicemen and Women's Association was founded in Britain in the 1970s. Since then the organisation has made great efforts to raise awareness of their contributions to the war (see Appendix I). Regarding the RAF, while black flyers were a minority among aircrew, they did make an important contribution to the British war effort, as this book will show. Exact figures have been difficult to establish, but in a memorandum prepared for the Air Ministry in 1945, an estimate of around 422 'coloured' (the blanket term then used to include West Indian, West African, and South Asian flyers) had served as aircrew during the war, with a further 3,900 acting as ground crew (see Statistics).[3]

When Britain declared war on Germany on 3 September 1939, the colonies rallied to support the war effort. For some it was an opportunity to show their loyalty to the mother country. For others, especially those who volunteered for the RAF, it was a chance to leave home and have an adventure. For the more progressive-thinking colonials, the war was seen as a route to post-war decolonisation and independence. Ben Bousquet, co-author of *West Indian Women at War*, said: 'Before the war, in all of the islands of the Caribbean, people were agitating for freedom. With the advent of war they put aside their protestations, they put aside their battles with the British government, and went to sign on to fight.'

In BBC Radio 2's documentary *The Forgotten Volunteers*, the presenter Trevor McDonald commented:

Altogether, over three and a half million black and Asian service personnel helped to win the fight for freedom but, despite the courage and bravery they showed in volunteering to fight, once the war was over, they found that old suspicions returned. Sometimes it's so easy to forget. To all the men and women from the West Indies, Africa and the Indian subcontinent, who volunteered to fight in the first and second world wars, we owe a debt of gratitude and respect.[4]

In 1974 BBC television screened a ground-breaking historical series called *The Black Man in Britain, 1550–1950*. It was the first British television programme to acknowledge that there had been a black community in Britain for over 400 years. One episode, 'Soldiers of the Crown', was the first to recognise the contribution made by West Indian servicemen to the Second World War. Two interviewees stood out, and they summarised the situation West Indians found themselves in after the declaration of war in 1939. They were Ivor Cummings, who had been the assistant welfare officer for the Colonial Office, and Dudley Thompson, a Jamaican who had served as a flight lieutenant in the RAF from 1941–45 and with the 49 Pathfinders Squadron. He was awarded several decorations. Towards the end of the war Thompson served as a liaison officer with the Colonial Office where he assisted Jamaican ex-servicemen who wanted to settle in London.

In 'Soldiers of the Crown', Ivor explained why he had been denied a commission in the RAF in 1939: 'That rule [in the King's Regulations] excluded all of us. I couldn't join the Royal Air Force because I was not of pure European descent. We were able to get rid of that ridiculous disqualification otherwise we should not have been able to mobilise our volunteers in the way that we did. They wouldn't have qualified for commissions.'[5] The rule referred to by Ivor was abandoned, but it was too late for Ivor who had accepted the post with the Colonial Office. He said: 'It is not done nowadays to talk about patriotism and the mother country because the Empire does not exist. It *did* exist in 1939 and there was no doubt at all that there was a great feeling of attachment and affection to this country by the colonies, in Africa and particularly in the West Indies.'[6]

Ivor said that one of the most important things that happened to West Indians during the war was the exposure to a different type of government, one that enabled them a certain amount of freedom, a better way of life and access to a higher education:

[S]o when they returned home after the war, they returned to the same government they had left. It was autocratic and people didn't want this. They resented this and the fact that the economic conditions in these places were absolutely appalling. For the returning servicemen and women, the officials, the governors, and others were very tiresome people indeed and didn't know how to deal with those who had been away in the war. After the war I was sent out to the Caribbean and I visited the three major islands, including Jamaica, and I was absolutely appalled. There were no opportunities for these people. The whole thing quite horrified me and I told everyone exactly what I felt about this. It was quite clear to me that this was a watershed. This whole war experience had been a watershed, that there were going to be changes.[7]

For many in the colonies post-war reform was slow, but the changes they expected eventually came with independence; for example, Ghana (1957), Nigeria (1960),

Jamaica (1962), Trinidad and Tobago (1962), Kenya (1963), Guyana (1966) and Barbados (1966).

In 'Soldiers of the Crown', Dudley Thompson described how he felt on arriving in England from Jamaica in 1940:

> As a colonial I would say the effect is confusing in that Jamaica – which you would consider a model colony – always saw the whites as leaders, governors, heads of departments, executives, and so on. You grew up with it. You knew that in the police force, no matter how great you were, you could never get promotion. Those were limitations you accepted. You weren't even militant about it. And then you come to a country where, for the first time, you see white street sweepers, white bus drivers and other more menial tasks that you never imagined white people did. It was an eye opener. Things were not as you had always expected it to be, and it was a psychologically traumatic situation and more than confusing.[8]

In England during the war, Dudley discovered that it was possible to meet – and make friends with – white people:

> You made friends, and you got used to the English way of life. There was a certain amount of courtesy from the English which you did not experience at home and you just adjusted into the English situation which was far from unpleasant. You were accepted as a soldier at a time when soldiers were coming from all parts of the Empire. You were rather proud that you wore a different flash on your shoulder because you saw Poland, France, Australia, Jamaica identified. You were just one of the sections of people whom England was glad to receive as fighting for the general cause.[9]

However, racial conflict was never far away:

> You'd find at dance halls there were incidents where they felt black soldiers should not be in that place and sometimes they came from people like the Rhodesian forces who were visiting as well. And you did find occasional cases of friction, so much so that towards the end of the war, liaison officers were created within the Royal Air Force to take care of these situations. I was a liaison officer and from time to time was called to various places where there were disruptions, fights, and ugly incidents that needed smoothing out.[10]

In Jamaica, access to education was restricted, but in wartime Britain Dudley discovered a whole new world of knowledge opened up to him:

> In the colonies there was very limited reading material; most of the books that would be interesting were banned anyway. There was no university. You come

to England and find you've got a far more liberal selection of material. You can walk into any library and pursue studies. You can pursue studies of your own country much more widely than you could at home.[11]

In 'Soldiers of the Crown', Dudley summarised the effect the war had on the colonials:

The effect on the armed forces, and the civilians who were munitions workers, was to show that, in England, while you were treated as a normal, average citizen, there were many more opportunities which were open to you there than were open to you at home. You could learn skills, at universities and technical schools, and you became proficient in those skills. Those skills were either non-existent at home or reserved for white people who were ruling you rather than for yourself. So to a great extent it tremendously increased your self-reliance. The other experience was to show that you were a foreigner and that when you went home you would have to be master in your own house. I would say it increased your sense of national feeling and for the first time you felt that you had to make your own home your own. You also met people from other parts of the Empire who felt similarly, particularly from Africa.[12]

The freedom that the British have enjoyed since 1945 was made possible by the support of the peoples of their former empire. These people made a major contribution to the winning of that freedom. They fought hard for it, and some even gave their lives. However, recognition for this support – and the sacrifices made – has been almost non-existent. In 1995 Britain's Conservative government, under the leadership of Prime Minister John Major, failed to invite any East and West African and Caribbean governments to take part in the fiftieth anniversary Victory in Europe (VE) Day celebrations on 8 May. Lobbying by the Black and Asian Studies Association (BASA) prompted Bernie Grant MP to take up the issue, and Marika Sherwood explained in her passionate editorial in BASA's Newsletter:

In what seems like something of a panic measure, the government took a partial U-turn: it invited the Jamaican and Trinidadian governments to participate. From what we understand, the other Caribbean governments were not consulted about this game of favouritism/imperialism. The information I have is that the largest number of servicemen/women who came to Britain from the Caribbean were from Jamaica, then British Guiana, Trinidad, Barbados, Bermuda. Bernie Grant declared himself to be satisfied with this outcome, but we were not. However, all further efforts met with rebuff; even our letter to the Queen as head of the Commonwealth only elicited the usual response from the Foreign and Commonwealth Office: insufficient numbers of Africans had actually fought in Europe. That the first victory over the Axis powers, the Italians in Abyssinia, which surely was the necessary precursor to the victories in Europe, had been fought partly by African troops was of no consequence. We also raised the issue of merchant seamen, up to one quarter of whom were from the colonial empire during the war: they have been completely ignored. Without the sacrifice of those men, so many of whom died, this country would have been starved both of food and of war material. So much for the grateful ex-Mother Country.[13]

Nine years later the historian Ray Costello offered an explanation for this omission when he was interviewed by the reporter Danielle Weekes in *The Voice* newspaper. He said that Britain had been reluctant to show the world that black servicemen and women from Britain and the colonies had played a part in freeing the oppressed 'because they were afraid that it would feed the desire for independence':

> If black people are shown to have the capacity for bravery it makes them human, heroes even. And heroes should have freedom and independence. Britain did not want that. It was more difficult to conceal our contributions at the end of World War II because of the sheer numbers who fought. The omission of the contribution of blacks to the British armed services is a crime comparable to slavery.[14]

Notes

1   Ken Follett, *Hornet Flight* (Macmillan, 2002), p. 9.

2   Sources: David Brewster, *Trinidad Express*, 25 January 2004; www.ken-follett. com.

3   NA AIR 2/6876, 'Coloured RAF Personnel: Report on Progress and Suitability', n.d. [Feb 1945]. See also AIR 2/6876, 'List of Colonial Aircrew', n.d.

4   *The Forgotten Volunteers*, BBC Radio 2, 11 November 2000.

5   'Soldiers of the Crown', *The Black Man in Britain, 1550–1950*, BBC2, 6 December 1974.

6   Ibid.

7   Ibid.

8   Ibid.

9   Ibid.

10   Ibid.

11   Ibid.

12   For more information about Ivor Cummings, see Stephen Bourne, *Mother Country: Britain's Black Community on the Home Front, 1939–45* (The History Press, 2010); and for more information about Dudley Thompson, see Dudley Thompson, *From Kingston to Kenya: The Making of a Pan-Africanist Lawyer* (The Majority Press, 1993). Thompson died at the age of 95 in New York City on 20 January 2012.

13 Marika Sherwood, *Black and Asian Studies Association Newsletter*, No. 12, April 1995, p. 3.

14 Ray Costello (interviewed by Danielle Weekes) in 'War of Words (60 years after D-Day, history must be rewritten to include tales of black servicemen)', *The Voice*, 31 May 2004, pp. 12–13.

PART I

BRITAIN

CHAPTER 1
'JOE' MOODY: AN OFFICER & AN ENGLISHMAN

In the late 1930s the British Army's adjutant general, Sir Robert Gordon-Finlayson, had recommended to the Army Council that commissions for all the armed services should be reserved for British subjects of British parents of pure European descent. However, when it became law, the Colonial Office was given the job of accommodating black Britons and West Indians who wished to fight the Nazis when the war broke out. They wrote to the War Office to have the law changed. The War Office replied that it was considering this 'thorny problem', but British policy towards colonial volunteers remained equivocal. A Foreign Office memo dispatched to colonial governors stated: 'We must keep up the fiction of there being no colour bar. Only those with special qualifications are likely to be accepted.'[1] Whitehall's reluctance to accept volunteers dated back to the First World War but, as the war escalated, Britain turned once more to its black subjects, including those in the Caribbean and other colonies, for support.

When the war broke out, Charles Arundel Moody, known as 'Joe', aged 22, qualified for basic training as an officer in the British Army. He had been educated at Alleyn's public school in Dulwich. The only black man to be commissioned as an officer in the British Army before then had been Walter Tull in 1917.[2] Joe went to a recruiting office in Whitehall for an interview but was dismayed when he was turned away on the grounds that officers in the British Army had to be of 'pure European descent'. Joe had a Jamaican father and an English mother. However, Joe's father, Dr Harold Moody, was no ordinary Jamaican. Dr Moody had settled in Britain in the Edwardian era and by 1939 was a highly respected community leader. The League of Coloured Peoples (LCP), which he had founded in 1931, had quickly established itself as the most influential organisation campaigning for the rights of black people in pre-war Britain.[3]

When Joe informed his father about his rejection from the army, an angry Dr Moody fought back. He contacted the Colonial Office and made an appointment with one of the undersecretaries. That meeting started the process which led to the Army Act being changed. Dr Moody and other members of the LCP joined forces with the International African Service Bureau (IASB) and the West African Students' Union (WASU) to lobby the government. Consequently, on 19 October 1939 the Colonial Office issued the following statement: 'British subjects from the colonies and British protected persons in this country, including those who are not of European descent, are now eligible for emergency commissions in His Majesty's Forces.' But Dr Moody remained unsatisfied. 'We are thankful for this,' he said, but 'we do not want it only for the duration of the war. We want it for all time. If the principle is accepted now, surely it must be acceptable all the time.'[4] Dr Moody and the LCP emphasised that they would not be satisfied by concessions in individual cases. He said:

> May I make myself and the position of the League quite clear? We are not seeking for specialist treatment in every case. We are merely seeking to establish our spiritual, cultural and mental equality, as members of the British Empire, with every other member of the Empire and to embody the term 'British Citizen' with some meaning and some reality as far as we are concerned. We claim the right to that freedom, which is the cherished possession of every Englishman and that no discrimination whatsoever should be made against us, except on the grounds of character and qualification. We are proud of our heritage and do not want to be subjected to any experience, which will in any way tend to rob us of that pride or which will cast a slur thereupon.[5]

Soon afterwards the army began to make exceptions. Commissions as lieutenants were granted to Dr Otto Wallen of Trinidad and Dr A. Marsh of Jamaica in the Royal Army Medical Corps, and Joe Moody was admitted to an officers' training unit. A Colonial Office minute in December 1939 recorded:

> Dr Moody's son is just off to Dunbar to join an officers training unit there – this does not ... amount to the definite grant of a commission, but it does mean that we have been able to secure a commission for Dr Moody's son in the unit as a special arrangement, since normally such units are now only recruited from men who have previously served for a period in the ranks.[6]

Joe was sent to Dunbar in Scotland where he joined an officer-cadet training unit: 'I went through four months of intense training where, because I was literally a guinea pig, I had to be very careful and mind my p's and q's and really perform outstandingly. I didn't get thrown out so I guess they thought I could make it.'[7] On the completion of his training, Joe was commissioned into the Queen's Own Royal West Kent Regiment.

As the war intensified, and with inadequate manpower available, Britain turned to its colonies and appealed to both white *and* black colonial subjects to bolster military ranks. The need for black recruits became more urgent in 1940 after the Fall of France (and the loss of British troops at Dunkirk) and the Battle of Britain. There was uneasiness about recruiting black colonials because a feeling of nationalism had grown in the colonies in the 1930s; yet most colonial soldiers remained loyal to the mother country as they had done in the past, such as when they gave support during the First World War.

In 1942, on his way to a posting in Kenya, Joe stopped off in South Africa with five white officers:

We did a two-day trip up to Durban and I walked around Durban and we really didn't run into any serious problem there. One of the officers would always go in first and explain they had a coloured British officer with them. We only ran into problems when we got to the Durban Country Club. We went there for tea one afternoon and the Secretary of the Club said, 'This is a private Club and it is a little peculiar. If you want to have tea, come and have it in my rooms.' So we left the Club very rapidly and went somewhere else. From there the six of us went up to Kenya and of course arriving in Kenya put the cat among the pigeons because African soldiers in Kenya were not allowed to speak English. Officers had to learn Swahili. So there was I, a coloured officer. They didn't like this at all. So after a very short time they shipped me over to Madagascar to get me out of the way.[8]

After two years in Madagascar and Egypt, Joe was posted to Italy to rejoin the Royal West Kent Regiment. When he arrived, a brigadier from headquarters came to see him. He told Joe that the Caribbean Regiment[9] had arrived in Italy and they needed company commanders:

I told him I would prefer to go up to the line with my own regiment. We had two battalions in Italy at the time but his will prevailed and I ended up with the Caribbean Regiment. Naturally I threw in my lot with them and I became a Jamaican. We underwent training in Egypt. Very intense. They thought that the West Indies would be good as night soldiers. The regiment that I had left in England did go into action in Europe and I would have preferred to stay with them.[10]

Joe became a major while he was serving in Egypt in 1945. At the end of the war he settled in Jamaica with B Company of the Caribbean Regiment. In 1947 his father died in London. Thousands of people paid their respects at Dr Moody's funeral which was held at the Camberwell Green Congregational Church. Professor David Killingray later explained that, during the war, by gradual pressure, Dr Moody and the LCP changed the attitude of government towards the recruitment of black servicemen and women, 'and to make them aware there is a question to be dealt with. The fact that they are dealt with much later perhaps owes something to Moody's pressure and his vision of a multi-racial Britain that he wanted.'[11]

After the war Joe Moody remained in the army and became a colonel in 1961. He was awarded the OBE in 1966 as the first commanding officer (CO) of the Jamaican Territorial Army. In 1990 he reflected on his experiences of the war:

My personal feeling – when I got rejected [in 1939] – was one of great disappointment, but I obviously had been born in Britain and, as far as I was concerned, I was an Englishman. I had all the necessary qualifications and there was my country wanting young men to do a job. There I was, fit and well, being turned down, so I was disappointed, but I can tell you, I stuck out my chest when I was commissioned in the British Army. I was flying in the air. I was very proud that I represented the colonies as a pioneer.[12]

Joe died on 11 January 2009 at the age of 91 in West Palm Beach, Florida.

Notes

1 Charles 'Joe' Moody, *Lest We Forget*, Channel 4, 8 November 1990.
2 Walter Tull was commissioned as a second lieutenant in the Middlesex Regiment on 30 May 1917. He thus became the first black/mixed race combat officer in the British Army, despite the 1914 Manual of Military Law specifically excluding 'Negroes/Mulattoes' from exercising actual command as officers. Tull's superior officers recommended him for a commission regardless.
3 For more information about Dr Harold Moody, see Stephen Bourne, *Dr. Harold Moody* (Southwark Council, 2008) and *Mother Country: Britain's Black Community on the Home Front, 1939–45* (The History Press, 2010). See also Professor David Killingray, 'Harold Moody (1882–1947)', *Oxford Dictionary of National Biography* (Oxford University Press, 2004; www.oxforddnb.com).
4 Moody, *Lest We Forget*.
5 Ibid.
6 Richard Hart, *Towards Decolonisation: Political, Labour and Economic Developments in Jamaica 1938–1945* (Canoe Press: University of the West Indies, 1999), p. 141.
7 Moody, *Lest We Forget*.
8 Ibid.
9 The Caribbean Regiment – also known as the Carib Regiment – was formed in the Second World War. The regiment went overseas in July 1944 and saw active service in the Middle East and Italy.
10 Moody, *Lest We Forget*.
11 *Hidden History: Dr Harold Moody*, BBC4/BBC Knowledge, 25 September 2000.
12 Moody, *Lest We Forget*.

CHAPTER 2

SID GRAHAM:
THE CALL OF THE SEA

Young Sid Graham dreamed of following in his father's footsteps and going to sea, and at the age of 15 he fulfilled his ambition and became a galley boy on the *Nernta*, a ship sailing to South America. From the 1930s to the 1950s Sid worked as a stoker on cargo boats operating from London. During the war Sid served as a merchant seaman (stoker) on Atlantic and Arctic convoys. It was dangerous work for it was the merchant seamen who suffered the most from the German U-boat attacks. By the end of 1940, 6,000 merchant seamen had been killed. In 1941 7,000 more lost their lives, and in 1942 8,000 perished. In total, more than 50,000 British merchant seamen died as a result of enemy action in the Second World War. Sid remembered: 'You was always on edge. You could never settle down. If you were sleeping you always got something on your mind – like torpedoes. But you knew what you had signed on for when you went on the ship.'[1]

Sid Graham was born in Tidal Basin, Custom House, in London's East End in 1920. He was the son of Sidney 'Siddy' Graham, a seaman from Barbados, and his English wife, an East Ender called Emma. In an interview with the local historian Howard Bloch in 1993, Sid remembered that racism – or the 'colour bar' as it was then known – was an issue in Britain when he was growing up, except in his own community: 'Canning Town, Tidal Basin, and Custom House, they were cosmopolitan, everybody lived round here: Africans, West Indians, Japanese, Chinese. Everybody got on.'[2]

At the beginning of 1942 Sid's worst fears were realised. He was crossing the Atlantic on a supply ship, the *Scottish Star*, when a German torpedo struck:

> I was having a bath in a bucket and when we got torpedoed I went up in the air and hit my ribs on the washbasin … busted 'em … I got up on the companionway and that's when the submarine started to shell us. Wasn't going down quick enough for him. I was badly hit in the arm. I went in the lifeboat and we got away from the ship and the ship went down … Luckily enough we were in the Caribbean, not in the cold, but we didn't know where we were going.[3]

The shipwrecked crew had no idea where they were because their voyage was a 'special operation'. Sid survived for ten days in the lifeboat with twenty other crew members.

On the lifeboat drinking water was strictly rationed and sharks could be seen in the sea: 'They used to come and float around … give you a look. And you'd make a noise and beat the sides of the boat with the oar and they'd float away. They can't stand noise we was told, so that's what we done. Happily it worked.'[4]

In 2005, when *The Newham Mag* published a VE Day special edition to commemorate the sixtieth anniversary of the end of the war, they featured Sid and described his experiences on the lifeboat: 'They were tossed around the Atlantic Ocean, suffering from severe cold and sea-sickness and existing on meagre daily rations of four fluid ounces of water and a couple of dry biscuits. When the men were picked up by a fishing boat from Barbados, they realised they had drifted into the Caribbean.'[5]

The fishing boat took Sid and the other survivors to Barbados. After landing, the local newspaper, *Barbados Advocate*, reported the story on its front page (28 February 1942), along with a photograph of the survivors who were named. The survivors were taken to the seaman's mission, but Sid and his colleagues were 'devastated' when their pay was stopped: 'in those days as soon as you got torpedoed on them ships your money was stopped right away … Only thing they give us was our clothes … we couldn't walk about *naked*, could we. It's hard to think what you been through and what you were doing … and they treat you like that.'[6]

Sid had never visited Barbados before but his father had come from the island and he had relatives there, although Sid had never met them. Eventually, Sid's Aunt Dorothy was located and she took him in. However, being wartime there was no way of letting his family know he was safe, and six months passed before a ship arrived to take him back to Britain. There were tears of joy when Sid was reunited with his parents and five younger siblings. 'My mother, God rest her soul, had been going crazy when I was away,' he later said.

While Sid had been in Barbados, his family had lost their London home in an air raid. They were rehoused, but Sid didn't know anything about it:

When I came home, I couldn't find them! So I went to the police station in Landsdowne Road to make enquiries, and I'm walking along with me suitcase, and my mother was scrubbing the step of the house opposite the police station. 'Siddy!' she shouted out to my Dad, 'Daddy! Sidney's here!' And they all came out to welcome me home. But afterwards the police thought I was a deserter and Mum done her nut. Then they came and took me to work on special operational jobs all through the rest of the war. I went to every invasion there was. I won all the medals, including the Burma Star, but I had to send ten shillings for every medal I won, but I gave them all to my children. Every time they did well at swimming my wife stitched the ribbons to their shorts![7]

In 1944 Sid took part in the D-Day landings in Normandy:

> We had to tow the ships out and then the engineers sunk 'em to make a mobile harbour. People think I'm lying but the first thing that landed on Normandy beaches was thousands of dogs to set off the mines. I wouldn't lie coz I was there. And yet if they'd told people that, there would have been uproar, never mind about men being blown up! It's been kept quiet. As we was going in, the Germans were dive bombing us, and a big yankee ship came along beside us for protection and they got hit.[8]

After the war ended in 1945, Sid continued to go to sea:

> You really looked forward to coming home to see your wife and your children … it's like being born again when you come home, everything's lovey-dovey. I'd be shovelling the coal in that furnace, couldn't put it in fast enough to get home, and I'd always bring them presents – bring them monkeys, canaries, parrots, dolls for the girls. They'd always expect something and they'd run up to me and hug me. When I left I used to kiss the kids, but I wouldn't let them see me to the door – just walk away, otherwise you'd get real melancholy. It's a terrible feeling when you're leaving, you feel downhearted.[9]

Sid signed off after one of his daughters was born. He stayed home for a couple of years and then decided to go to sea again:

> I was at sea when my son was born but my wife wasn't allowed to send me a telegram. Officers were privileged, and could receive telegrams from their wives when their children were born, but we were discriminated against. As you drop down in rank you don't get the privileges. We had to do all the donkey work to make the steam to make the ship move. And when you wasn't doing that, you mended something, you were always doing something. And when your watch had finished, you had to go and mend the winches and all that. You were never at rest, you were always doing something. It was a hard life, I tell yer. If a man was sick, you had to go down and do his work. I finished working on the ships about 1956. We had children, and I wasn't seeing them. The wife said it was no life for them, so I quit. I went and got a job in the dock and settled down. My family came first. All my sons and daughters have been good to me. I haven't got a dodgy one.[10]

Notes

1   Steve Humphries, 'Sailors at War', *The Call of the Sea: Britain's Maritime Past 1900–1960* (BBC Books, 1997), pp. 119–21.

2 Sid Graham interviewed by Howard Bloch at the Cundy Centre, Hartington Road, Custom House, 7 October 1993. Used with Mr Bloch's permission.

3 *The Call of the Sea.*

4 Ibid.

5 'All at sea in battle for survival', *The Newham Mag* (VE Day Special), 7 May 2005.

6 *The Call of the Sea.*

7 Interview with Howard Bloch.

8 Ibid.

9 *The Call of the Sea.*

10 Interview with Howard Bloch.

CHAPTER 3

LILIAN & RAMSAY BADER: LIFE IN THE FORCES

Lilian Bader is proud of the fact that, by the end of the twentieth century, three generations of her family had served in the British armed services:

A father in the First World War, his only three children in the Second World War, and then I married a coloured man who was in the Second World War, as was his brother who was even decorated for bravery in Burma. And their father had been in the First World War. And our son was a helicopter pilot, he served in Northern Ireland. So all in all, I think we've given back more to this country than we've received.[1]

Lilian was born in the Toxteth Park area of Liverpool in 1918. Her father, Marcus Bailey, was a Barbadian who had served in the merchant navy during the First World War. Lilian was the youngest of three children, but after they were orphaned she was separated from her brothers and raised in a convent. Lilian remained there until she was 20 because no one would employ her. There were no other black children at the convent but Lilian possessed a strong personality. She was determined to overcome prejudice and later said she had always been a bit rebellious: 'take me as you find me and if you don't like me, too bad!'[2] As a teenager Lilian proved to be popular with her classmates and was often top of her class. She made numerous attempts to secure a job and often experienced racism at job interviews: 'Nobody would employ me, and that was when I realised I had a problem with colour.'[3]

Lilian eventually found employment in domestic service but, when the war broke out, she was determined to support the war effort. An opportunity came with the Navy, Army and Air Force Institutes (NAAFI) at Catterick Camp, Yorkshire, but it didn't last long. Though Lilian worked hard she was shocked when she was asked to leave. Her father's West Indian background had been discovered and, in spite of the efforts of the NAAFI staff to keep her, she lost the job because of the 'colour bar' in the armed services that existed at the start of the war.

Lilian returned to domestic service but she was determined to join up. In 1940 she heard a group of West Indians on the radio. They told the interviewer they had been rejected by the army but recruited into the RAF. Lilian decided to try for a position in the air force and was thrilled when, on 28 March 1941, she was recruited by the WAAF, though she found herself 'the only coloured person in this sea of white faces'.[4] Lilian's joy at being enlisted, however, was overshadowed by tragedy. Her brother, Able Seaman James Bailey, was killed in action on 14 March 1941 while serving in the merchant navy. Despite this, in December 1941 Lilian became a leading aircraftwoman (LACW) and soon gained the rank of acting corporal.

Through an ex-landlady in Yorkshire, Lilian made contact with a young British-born black soldier called Ramsay Bader. He was a tank driver who was serving with the 147th (Essex Yeomanry) Field Regiment, Royal Artillery. He was the son of a soldier from Freetown, Sierra Leone, and an English mother, but had been adopted at the age of six months and raised by a white family. Lilian and Ramsay exchanged letters and photographs:

Even in the ugly khaki battle dress, he looked like an officer. However, I remembered the old adage, 'good looking nowt,' and reserved judgement. When my sister-in-law asked me later what I thought, I said he was one of those 'actually' men, in what I thought was a drawling RP accent [received pronunciation, which means the old-style 'BBC English' without regional accents]. We both had religious backgrounds; his was Methodist though his parents had become Quakers. His voice was low, practically without an accent, and he did not swear or say anything which would destroy the respectable image I had formed. It was a relief to meet a coloured boy-friend for a change. I had met no other coloured WAAFs, and only seen an Indian RAF officer and one coloured airman who appeared fleetingly at Condover.[5]

Following her marriage to Ramsay in 1943, Lilian's chances of further promotion in the WAAF were curtailed when she discovered she was expecting a baby. She received her discharge in February 1944.

Interviewed by Conrad Wood for the Imperial War Museum in 1989, Ramsay explained that he had been born in Chiswick in 1919. His adopted father was Ernst Bader, a German-Swiss businessman who had settled in England and become a naturalised Englishman. Ramsay took his adopted father's surname and was raised in Stanford le Hope in Essex: 'After the war I found out that I had an older brother and we met up. He had served in Burma during the war, but our mother had died, so I never met her. I learned that our father had served in the First World War.'[6]

When Ramsay left school at the age of 16, in spite of having achieved good qualifications, he faced difficulty finding a job because of his colour: 'So my adopted father sent me to Stratford to work in one of his factories. I stayed there until I got my calling up papers for the army in 1939.'[7] Ramsay said that when the war broke out, he was aware of Hitler's attitude to black people because he remembered Hitler's appalling treatment of the African American athlete Jesse Owens at the 1936 Olympics in Berlin:

Why should human beings be treated like that when the Olympics is for sport for every nationality? I couldn't understand it and it made me want to fight against this sort of thing because having read what Hitler was doing to the Jews, the coloured would be next for the gas chamber. I was born in Britain and accepted it as my country and I must fight for what I believe in, which I still think today. I did the right thing. During the war there was a friendly attitude from most service people and I didn't feel too much prejudice because we were all fighting for the same cause. But after the war nobody wanted to employ us. And yet I'd served my country, but at least now, looking back over the years, I am glad I met other coloureds and met other people who all fought for the same cause. My brother was a sergeant major, decorated, and we served with all the other people who fought for the survival of mankind.[8]

On 6 June 1944, Ramsay was one of thousands of soldiers engaged in the D-Day landings:

We felt very sick, having not experienced this type of heavy swell which you get in the Channel, and the terrible loss of life, seeing floating bodies who had been hit by shells that had come in from the enemy. Although resistance from the enemy wasn't supposed to be very strong we still met quite strong pockets of resistance.[9]

Ramsay discovered that the French people they were helping to liberate were not always very friendly towards the British soldiers,

...because they remembered Dunkirk in 1940, and they were not sure if we were going to be pushed back into the sea again. German sniping was always there. But the Free French and the resistance always helped us. Finally we made for the town of Bayeux. With the Americans on our right and the Canadians further down all these helped to form a bridgehead which was finally held.[10]

It was an anxious time for Lilian and she prayed that her husband would survive, which Ramsay did. He left the army in 1945. In spite of the fact that they had been born in Britain, and had served their king and country during the war, the couple faced discrimination in employment after the war, but Lilian was always determined to improve her education. In the 1960s she attended evening classes and, after graduating, trained for a teaching certificate. As a teacher she mainly worked in schools and colleges in the Bournemouth area until she retired in 1984. Ramsay died in 1992 at the age of 73. In 2008, at the age of 90, Lilian travelled to London for the opening of the Imperial War Museum's 'From War to Windrush' exhibition (see Appendix II).

Notes

1   Jacine Cooper, 'Lilian M. Bader – Leading Aircraftwoman', www.bgfl.org.
2   Ibid.
3   Ben Bousquet and Colin Douglas, *West Indian Women at War: British Racism in World War II* (Lawrence and Wishart, 1991), p. 17.
4   Lilian Bader, *Together: Lilian Bader: Wartime Memoirs of a WAAF 1939–1944* (Imperial War Museum, 1989), p. 5
5   Ibid., p. 9.
6   Ramsay Bader, interviewed by Conrad Wood for the Imperial War Museum, 15 January 1989. Reference 10593.
7   Ibid.
8   Ibid.
9   Ibid.
10 Ibid.

CHAPTER 4

AMELIA KING & THE WOMEN'S LAND ARMY

Shortly before the outbreak of war, the Ministry of Agriculture decided to recreate the Women's Land Army – a throwback to the First World War. By August 1939 the Women's Land Army had 30,000 recruits. However, in 1943, when Amelia King, a young black woman who was born in 1917 in Limehouse in the East End of London, volunteered to join, she was turned down. Her father, Henry King, from British Guiana, had served in the merchant navy, and her brother, Fitzherbert, was serving in the Royal Navy. Amelia was rejected by the Essex County Committee because she was black. It was claimed that some farmers had objected to employing her. Consequently, Amelia's predicament was debated in the House of Commons.[1]

When Amelia's story was highlighted in several newspapers, it aroused feelings of anger in many British people who felt that it was wrong for a country to racially discriminate while fighting Hitler and fascism. Further evidence of support for Amelia showed in a poll carried out by the public opinion organisation Mass Observation. It stated that 49 per cent of the 62 per cent who had heard about Amelia 'strongly disapproved' of the act of racism, while a further 12 per cent 'disapproved': 'A rider was added that "even those who did not entirely believe in colour equality were against this particular case of colour prejudice which was regarded as detrimental to the war effort".'[2]

Amelia's story has been mentioned in several books, including Peter Fryer's *Staying Power: The History of Black People in Britain*, but what happened to her *after* the racist incident has never been researched or documented, until now. Although no record has come to light of Amelia's point of view, farmer Alfred Roberts, of Frith Farm in Fareham, Hampshire, explained in his unpublished memoir that in 1943, because of the war, he had lost a number of his regular staff:

> So I had these delightful Land Army girls around me who were so willing and so happy to work under the leadership of my daughter Betty. I think, about this time, a photograph of a black girl in a field appeared, as a cartoon, and underneath was the inscription, 'All God's Children'. This girl was refused entry into the Women's Land Army as she was coloured. This appeared in the *Daily Express* newspaper. So I immediately wrote up the Editor and offered to take this

poor black girl. They sent a representative from the *Daily Express* to interview me and I stated that I had no colour prejudice and I wished to take this girl, Amelia King. I was not seeking publicity but I found myself the hero of the hour and a Welsh poet published a poem entitled 'Christian Farmer'. People came to interview me from all over the place. Eventually Amelia King appeared and I rigged her up with a uniform although the Land Army refused to have her. I had in the ranks of the Land Army a good-natured girl called Jessie and she took Amelia King around to all the pubs in the neighbourhood where Jessie and Amelia were the heroines of the hour. This caused more publicity.

In a letter to the author, Mr Roberts' granddaughter Hazel explains that her mother, Betty, remembers Amelia as 'a young lady determined to do her bit for the war effort':

Regrettably, as I am sure was the case with other young women who joined the Women's Land Army, she did not realise how hard the work would be, nor how terribly monotonous, though my mother recalls she did work at Frith Farm for about a year [1943–44]. My grandfather's character – as both my mother and I remember him and more potently may be gathered from his memoirs – was dynamic, energetic, forward-thinking, and charismatic. His attitude to life was 'absolutely can do'. He refused to accept defeat on any problem, no matter how insurmountable it first appeared to be. He thrived on challenge. A great 'people person' he was much loved by those who worked for him for his unorthodox approach to life, his boundless enthusiasm, his practical jokes and his great sense of humour.[3]

Amelia King, a retired fancy-box maker, died in the Royal London Hospital in Whitechapel in 1995 at the age of 78.

Notes

1   For further information see Peter Fryer, *Staying Power: The History of Black People in Britain* (Pluto Press, 1984), p. 364; *Parliamentary Debates*, 5th series, Vol. 392 (1943), cols 390–1.

2   Graham A. Smith, 'Jim Crow on the Home Front (1942–1945)', *New Community*, Winter 1980, Vol. 3, p. 325.

3   With thanks to Naomi Benson (Lion TV); genealogist Megan Owens; and Hazel Luetchford (letter to Stephen Bourne, 9 January 2012).

CHAPTER 5
MUSICIANS IN BATTLEDRESS

RAY ELLINGTON

When the war began the world of show business provided the armed services with a number of recruits; one of them was the drummer Ray Ellington. He was born Harry Brown in London in 1916 and took his professional surname from the American jazz giant Duke Ellington. He had his first break in show business in 1937 when he joined Harry Roy and his Orchestra. He joined the RAF in May 1940 and served until his demobilisation in 1946. In the RAF Ellington reached the rank of flight sergeant as a physical training instructor and he taught unarmed combat to officer trainees. He also took up driving articulated vehicles, carrying bombs and gliders to Scotland and back to London. He managed to revert to his previous trade as a musician during the last year of his service by playing in various service bands, including the RAF Blue Eagles, and playing for the Entertainments National Service Association (ENSA). After the war, Ellington found fame with his popular jazz quintet and then as a member of the team of BBC radio's popular *Goon Show* (1951–60). He died in 1985.[1]

GEOFF LOVE

Geoff Love was born in Yorkshire in 1917. He started playing the trombone at the age of 11, which he virtually taught himself. After leaving school at 14 he gigged with little bands around his birthplace, Todmorden, while working as a motor mechanic. In February 1940 he received his call-up papers and joined the King's Royal Rifle Corps. After his initial training he helped to re-form the Green Jackets' regimental dance band. During six years' military service he taught himself orchestration and on his demobilisation worked as a freelance trombonist and arranger.[2] From the end of the war until his death in 1991, Love was one of Britain's most popular and prolific easy-listening orchestra leaders. In the 1950s and '60s he worked with many great singers, including Paul Robeson, Judy Garland and Shirley Bassey.

FRANK HOLDER

Born in 1925 in Georgetown, British Guiana, Holder began singing as a child at church socials. He volunteered for the RAF in 1944 and later told Mark Gardner in *Jazz Journal* (July 2010):

> It was towards the end of the war, but many of the young men in the West Indies wanted to help Britain's fight. You have to remember that at that time everyone out there regarded Britain as the mother country, it was a big deal; we were anxious to do our bit. I also wanted to be where the musical action was, ideally America, but that wasn't possible. Britain offered prospects and a challenge.

Holder crossed the Atlantic to Glasgow: 'It was a hairy crossing. A lot of U-boats were around, but we were well protected in a convoy. It was an exciting time and we were keen to get into the action, but as things turned out we were held in reserve and sat out the war in Wiltshire. As an AC2 a lot of my time was spent in the cookhouse!' Holder served in Britain until 1948. During this time he sang with various service groups, including the band at RAF Cranwell in Lincolnshire. While still in his RAF uniform, Holder sang at many popular entertainment venues in London, such as the Hammersmith Palais and the Lyceum Ballroom in The Strand. After demobilisation he joined Leslie 'Jiver' Hutchinson's jazz band and then found fame with John Dankworth's band (1950–56). Holder's singing and bongo playing became a great attraction and in 1951, when a young singer called Cleo Laine joined Dankworth's band, she was incorrectly advertised as a new kind of musical instrument – the Cleolaine – played by Holder! In 1958, after being named as one of Britain's most popular male vocalists by *Melody Maker*, Holder became a freelance entertainer and cabaret artiste, and in 2012 he celebrated his 87th birthday, still singing and swinging.

REGINALD FORESYTHE

After Reginald Foresythe's untimely death in 1958, obituaries celebrated him as one of the most innovative jazz composers of the 1930s. The jazz critic Charles Fox described Foresythe's music as frequently possessing wit, as well as sophistication, 'charm as well as ingenuity, and certainly nobody in this country worked harder to expand the boundaries of jazz'.[3] In 1941 Foresythe curtailed his illustrious career in jazz music to join the RAF, but after he died his RAF service was barely acknowledged.

Foresythe was born in the Shepherd's Bush area of London in 1907, the son of a Nigerian barrister and an Englishwoman. He received a public school education and throughout his life he used his upper-class British accent to achieve some measure of acceptance as a black Briton. In the 1930s in Britain he won respect in jazz circles for his bold and dazzling compositions, and among the most famous were 'Deep Forest', 'Serenade for a Wealthy Widow' and 'Dodging a Divorcee'.

When the American singer Elisabeth Welch made London her home in 1933 she was offered cabaret engagements but, she later recalled:

> I didn't know anyone who could accompany me. I was given Reggie's name and, of course, I'd heard about him in America and Paris. He was a sweet, simple, charming person. His appearance was always immaculate and elegant. He loved good food and talked with that wonderful English upper class accent. When we made fun of his accent, he didn't mind at all. He had a great sense of humour about himself. I used to go almost two or three times a week to see him perform his famous 'New Music' at the 400 Club, a very chic place in Leicester Square.[4]

A 'confirmed bachelor', no woman was ever romantically associated with him. Elisabeth said: 'His liaisons with other men were always very discreet.'

When the war broke out, Foresythe was overage for active service, but he volunteered for the RAF anyway. Drafted into the air force in 1941 with an officer's ranking, he became an intelligence officer and served at remote Scottish air bases and in North Africa. According to the jazz historian Val Wilmer, 'he had his battle-dress uniform tailored by his usual tailor. I believe that this was not all that unusual among officers, and those who could afford to do so opted for having a more comfortable uniform made. But I'm not sure whether it was permitted!'[5] As soon as he was demobbed in 1946, Foresythe sold his uniform: 'The purchaser was delighted, and amazed by both the tailoring and the quality of the material. He left his mark, remembered for addressing every airman, from commanding officer to newest recruit, as "dear boy".'[6]

In his civilian life and throughout his war service Foresythe had to conceal his homosexuality and, as his friend Elisabeth Welch stated, his liaisons with men had to be discreet. Male homosexuality remained a criminal offence in Britain until 1967. However, for the most part, it was unofficially tolerated in the armed services for the duration of the war. For some heterosexual servicemen, same-sex encounters were considered preferable to going to brothels and catching a sexually transmitted disease. Some gay men could be open and were protected by their comrades; others were considered good for morale and became 'mascots', but same-sex relationships were court-martial offences in the armed services and servicemen risked being kicked out if discovered.[7]

In the 1930s Foresythe had been ahead of his time, but after the war, time seemed to have passed him by. In the 1950s he was found leading bands in West Country hotels and playing solo piano in drinking clubs in London's Soho and Kensington. His career ended in obscurity and alcoholism, and he died from heart failure at the age of 51 after a fall at his home in London. After he died, the BBC producer John Burnaby told the *Melody Maker* (1 March 1959):

> Foresythe was to jazz what Stravinsky is to classical music. He was constantly changing in mood from the lush to the cheeky witty counterpoint of, for instance, 'Dodging a Divorcee'. As a person, he was without doubt the most lovable musician of his time. Witty, gay, imperturbable, he couldn't care less if he were rich or poor. Music was the most important thing in his life.

LESLIE THOMPSON

Trumpeter Leslie Thompson was born in Jamaica in 1901. He joined the band of the West India Regiment before coming to Britain in 1919 to train as a military bandsman at the Royal Military School of Music at Kneller Hall. In 1920 Thompson applied to be a bandmaster at Kneller Hall:

> I asked the Director ... and he advised me to talk it over with my Commandant in Kingston, whose recommendation would be necessary ... We got back to Kingston on Christmas Day, 1920 ... I told the lads that I wanted to be a Bandmaster, and they laughed; fetch a copy of the King's Regulations, they said. And there it plainly was written that anyone above the rank of Warrant Officer, Third Class, had to be European. After more than 60 years I still believe that the Kneller Hall Director told me that because he wanted to soften the blow, knowing that it would be easier for me to accept back in Jamaica.[8]

Thompson eventually settled in London in 1929 and continued his career as a musician. He toured Europe with Louis Armstrong in 1934–35, but they didn't make it to Germany because, Thompson recalled, 'Hitler didn't want his master race polluted by us'. Thompson formed his own band with the encouragement of the Guyanese dancer Ken 'Snakehips' Johnson. From 1937 until he was called up in 1942, Thompson played in a band led by Edmundo Ros:

> I was now 40, so the military weren't exactly that anxious to have me, but they needed people in the anti-aircraft defences, and so I got my call up papers for the Royal Artillery and off to Devizes I went ... At the station there was a three ton truck, and the Bombardier called out 'Anyone for Wiltshire Barracks?' and twenty or so of us stepped over. We got in the back and looked at each other, all wondering what would happen next. At the barracks we all got out, and were directed to a hut and told to pick out a bed. A chap came in and gave us a paper, telling us to fill in details of our education, civvy street job, and experience. After a while he collected them.[9]

Afterwards, Thompson was collected and taken to see the adjutant, Captain Ball, who shook his hand and invited him to take charge of their band: he described them as 'semi-pros'. So Thompson took over the band and discovered that his association with the famous bandleader Edmundo Ros helped to make him a popular figure at the camp. When Thompson served in the Royal Artillery he was accepted:

> I was a member of the artillery's Motor Transport division. There were thousands of troops in the area, and airforce too ... and there were the Wellington bombers which would fly off on bombing raids over Europe. There were plenty of instructors, old and experienced sergeants, and so the ignorant had little opportunity to show their stupidity. So there was no trouble over race.[10]

In 1943 Thompson was praised for shooting down the highest flying German plane over Britain:

> That Messerschmidt 109 G was seven miles up ... and everyone was interested. General Sir Frederick Pile came along: he was in charge of British anti-aircraft defences, and he came along with his brasshats. He was a very nice little man. As Sergeant, in charge of the team on the gun, I had to meet all these people, with the other Sergeants and their gunners. Of course none of us knew who had fired the shell, because we were all firing. So that was my moment of glory in the war.[11]

In 1944 Thompson was transferred to the Stars in Battledress (SiB), an organisation that produced entertainment during the war for and by military personnel. He stayed with SiB until his demobilisation in 1946: 'So I got transferred. I was still Sergeant Thompson, R.A., but now I lived out of barracks, as a sort of private soldier. We rehearsed a lot ... there were any number of bands by the end of 1944. My outfit was Latin American, and we dressed to suit this.'[12]

At the end of the war, in May 1945, Thompson visited Germany and Norway with SiB:

> In Germany the troops were absolutely isolated from the natives. There was a certain amount of tension and insecurity about the future, so the Germans were left alone and the troops were kept away. Physically Germany was a revelation, for as we flew over the cities which had been blitzed by the RAF you could see rubble, houses without roofs or windows, and rubble everywhere. It made you think that the Germans had started this war and had got the answer all right. Mind you, we didn't feel glad; or sorry, either.[13]

After the war, Thompson continued to perform as a musician in clubs and dance halls in London, but he ceased to work as a professional musician in 1954. Two years before he died, at the age of 86 in 1987, with the help of Jeffrey Green he published his autobiography. It was reprinted in 2009 as *Swing from a Small Island*.[14]

Notes

1 Val Wilmer, 'Ray Ellington (1916–1985)', *Oxford Dictionary of National Biography* (Oxford University Press, 2004; www.oxforddnb.com).

2 Val Wilmer, 'Geoff Love (1917–1991)', *Oxford Dictionary of National Biography* (Oxford University Press, 2004; www.oxforddnb.com).

3 Charles Fox, 'Home Cooking', *Just Jazz 3* (Four Square Books, 1959), p. 30.

4 Elisabeth Welch, interview with Stephen Bourne, London, 28 April 1995.

5 Val Wilmer, letter to Stephen Bourne, 20 October 2011.

6 Ibid.

7 Stephen Bourne, 'On the Same Side', *BBC History Magazine*, February 2012, pp. 30–1.

8 Leslie Thompson with Jeffrey Green, *Swing from a Small Island: The Story of Leslie Thompson* (Northway Publications, 2009), p. 35.

9 Ibid., pp. 105–6.

10 Ibid., pp. 107, 111–14.

11 Ibid., pp. 119–20.

12 Ibid., p. 121.

13 Ibid.

14 See also Val Wilmer, 'Leslie Thompson', *City Limits*, 13–19 December 1985, pp. 84–5.

PART II

GUYANA & THE CARIBBEAN

CHAPTER 6

CY GRANT: INTO THE WIND

When Cy Grant became a popular television personality in the 1950s and '60s, the British public was unaware that he had served in the RAF during the Second World War and had been a prisoner of war (POW).[1] It was his regular appearances singing topical news stories with a calypso beat in the BBC programme *Tonight* that made Cy a household name.

It would take until 2006, and the publication of Cy's war memoir, *'A Member of the RAF of Indeterminate Race'*, for a brief but fascinating account of his wartime experiences. In the title of the book, Cy refers to a caption for a photograph that had been taken of himself in the POW camp and then published in a German newspaper in 1943. This was intended as a propaganda exercise for the Nazis, suggesting that the situation was so bad in England that the RAF had resorted to recruiting people of unknown or 'indeterminate race' to fight in the war. However, there may have been an element of truth in the Nazis' thinking. In 1941, following the Fall of France and the Battle of Britain – and the loss of many lives – the RAF had had to change its mind about its discriminatory policy of barring black recruits. Finally, 'men of colour' were allowed into its privileged ranks and Cy was one of the first to be recruited as aircrew, as well as being commissioned as an officer.

Cy was born Cyril Grant in 1919 in British Guiana (known as Guyana after independence in 1966):

My father was a Moravian minister of African descent, my mother was Eurasian – her father was English and was connected with Nelson in some way. I was brought up in a typically colonial way, singing 'Rule Britannia' and learning about English history and geography, but not knowing anything about the country I was born in. I knew as a young person in Guyana that something was wrong. I didn't feel privileged, even though my family life was very privileged – we had servants for example. And, even as someone who was brought up to feel English and appreciate European music and Shakespeare, I felt frustrated with the colonial way of life. I knew that the colony was too small to hold me. I think that happened to lots of West Indians who had any kind of creative ability.[2]

Cy's father, who had been born in the Victorian era but had a very modern understanding of the dilemmas facing colonial society, nurtured in his son a love of books, as well as the importance of black figures in the development of western civilisation. He impressed upon his son that two nineteenth-century literary figures, the Russian Alexander Pushkin and the French Alexandre Dumas, were of mixed ancestry, and that Toussaint L'Ouverture, who led a revolution in Haiti, was a great black leader. Cy's father wanted him to go into the ministry, but Cy knew he had no specific calling for it, 'though I thought at one stage that I'd go into it because it would give me an opportunity to get a university education. But then the Second World War came and I applied for aircrew in the Royal Air Force.'[3]

In 1938 a friend of Cy's, Sydney Kennard, the son of an English doctor and his black wife, had applied to join the RAF but had been refused entry, even though he had been to America to study aviation and was given his pilot's licence. He paid his way back to England with the intention of joining up but they wouldn't accept him. That was just before they changed the policy:

> I was one of the first four people who joined the RAF from the colonies. They had just changed their policy towards recruiting black people, so that's how I got in. I trained as a pilot but then, half way through my training, I was switched to navigator. I didn't make anything of this at the time, because I did not realise that it was not above board. But, much later, I discovered through a friend that there were problems with the English aircrew not wanting to fly with black pilots. At one stage, I tried to get out of the RAF, but without success.[4]

Cy was posted to 103 Squadron based at RAF Elsham Wolds in Lincolnshire. He was a member of a mixed Canadian and British seven-man crew of a Lancaster bomber. He qualified as navigator and astronomical navigator on 5 February 1943. He later said, although it was almost impossible for a black recruit to be a pilot, he never experienced any racism in the RAF:

> I still had not been subjected to any form of overt prejudice. A war was on and I was wearing a uniform. People were generally friendly. In the streets I occasionally heard a child say 'Look, mummy, a black man!' That always brought me up sharp. Before coming to England I didn't think of myself as black – a quite salutary shock! I was to realize that I was defined in a certain way 'at home' and another in the 'mother country'. Coming to terms with either label was to realize that I was an outsider – that white people excluded people of any colour other than their own. On walking into a saloon bar in the country, suddenly there would be a deathly hush. It was as though I had suddenly come from an alien planet. Later, as an officer, there was a mild raising of eyebrows when I first walked into the mess, but this soon turned to acceptance when I spoke the King's English, albeit with my West Indian accent.[5]

Cy flew on bombing missions over the Ruhr and in June 1943 he was shot down over Holland on his third mission during the massive offensive over Germany. In 2008, at the age of 88, he described to Alec Lom in *The Telegraph* what happened:

We had successfully bombed Gelsenkirchen … when we came under attack as we flew home from Holland. The tail gunner, Pilot Officer Joe Addison, shouted over the intercom that a German fighter was closing in from underneath us. The German fired a long volley and a jet of tracer spat out towards us. Addison, from his tail turret, returned fire immediately. The fighter climbed a little and veered off to the right, bringing him into the field of fire of the mid-upper gunner, Sergeant Geoffrey Wallis, who immediately opened fire. Everything was happening very fast. All hell had broken loose. Flying Officer Alton Langille, the pilot, pushed the nose of the Lancaster into a dive, and in a moment the world turned upside down. Then, as suddenly as it all began, everything was normal again. The German fighter was nowhere to be seen. Our gunners must have shot it down! 'Great work, guys!' shouted the skipper, his voice betraying both the strain we were all under and the relief! He levelled out and the plane behaved normally. The pilot checked our position with me. Despite the evasive action, I had a good idea of where we should be – somewhere south of Amsterdam, near the small town of Haarlem. In half an hour we would be back. But our piece of mind was to be short-lived. This time it was the mid-upper gunner's voice over the intercom. 'Starboard outer afire, Skipper!' So we'd been hit after all! We dived steeply in an effort to smother the flames, but when we levelled out the flames had spread. Then one of the wheels of the undercarriage fell away in a flaming circle. Now we were up against it. By the time we reached the coast, we were a flaming comet over the Dutch sky. Both wings were on fire now and I gave the shortest course to the English coast. Unfortunately we were flying into a headwind of about 80 miles an hour at 20,000 feet. Undaunted, we had unanimously decided to risk getting across the Channel rather than turn back and bail out over occupied territory. But it was becoming extremely difficult for Al to control the aircraft and he sensed that we would not make it across the Channel. He decided to turn back over land.[6]

Al, the pilot, was forced to make a decision that would change Cy's life. With no other options available, he ordered his crew to bail out. Cy recalled that dramatic moment:

I had never contemplated being in this situation. We had been instructed in the use of parachutes but never had to practise leaving an aeroplane by one. When I went forward I found that the bomb aimer and engineer, who should have left in that order, were struggling to get through the hatch-door situated below the bomb aimer's cushion in the nose of the plane. Al left his controls and came after me.

The four of us were soon piled one on top of the other, tossed from side to side in the cramped space of the nose of the plane. Though not comprehending why we were unable to escape the now fiercely burning plane, I do not recall any sense of fear or panic. We seemed locked in a timeless moment of inertia when suddenly, with a deafening blast, which lit up everything, our aircraft blew up and disintegrated, freeing us from each other – a free-fall into eternity. My 'chute opened readily and I felt a sudden jerk and the strain of the harness on my shoulders as the wind snatched the canopy. I was swaying violently from side to side. Except for the rush of the wind I was now in an unreal world of mist and utter silence. To add to the unreality, it seemed as if I was suspended in the air, for at first I experienced no sensation of falling.[7]

Cy landed in a field south of Nieuw-Venneg and hid in a cornfield for most of the day, but two of the crew had been killed outright, including the Canadian tail gunner, Joe Addison. Cy was aware that Germans were searching for survivors of the crash. He had been instructed to escape to Spain but he realised that, as a black man in Occupied Europe, it would be impossible for him to undertake this task without attracting attention. His only hope was to seek help from the Dutch. In the early evening he attracted the attention of a farmer who took him to his farm, where his wife tended to a cut on his head and fed him. However, a local Dutch policeman had heard he was there and, after collecting Cy, handed him over to the Germans.

Cy was taken to an interrogation camp in Amsterdam and placed in solitary confinement for five days. A few days later he was transported with many other POWs to the camp known as Stalag Luft III (later the scene of *The Great Escape*), before being sent to another POW camp a few kilometres away. He later said: 'For the most part my captivity was painless. At least we were alive.'[8] There were no other black officers in the POW camp and Cy found that there was no obvious racism directed towards him:

[This was] because I was in a predominantly Canadian ('colonial') mess with Al, my pilot, being particularly popular and sought after, I basked in that popularity too. There was only one occasion I remember when an American airman called me a nigger! He was from the Deep South, I gathered, and just could not understand that I was an officer in the British Air Force.[9]

Cy's artistic talent proved useful in the POW camp:

The fellows used to bring me photographs of their girlfriends and I made portraits, enlargements, from these photographs, for a bar of chocolate or three packs of cigarettes. So we kept ourselves occupied. Everyone wanted to try and escape, and everyone was roped in, even just to keep an eye on the guards. There was always activity.[10]

As a prisoner of war, Cy discovered that he had a great deal of time to reflect on the direction of his life and on what he wanted to do after he was released:

> I met a lot of good people because, as an officer in the RAF, you were among the cream of officers. I met all sorts of people, including writers, schoolteachers, lecturers and scientists. And, living for two years close together, I learnt a great deal and asked a lot of questions – that's where I matured, actually. I decided then, that I would study law, because I wanted to go back to the Caribbean. My ambition was to help get the British out of the West Indies.[11]

Cy described the worst part of his imprisonment as occurring during the last few months of the war. The officers' POW camp where Cy had been imprisoned for two years was evacuated with the approach of the Soviet Army in early 1945: 'Forced marches in deep snow for days on end with little rations, sleeping in barns, then transported in cattle trucks jammed together like sardines in a tin.'[12] After days of trudging through snow, the prisoners found themselves in a lice-ridden POW camp at Lukenwalde, about 50km south of Berlin. As the war raged on, and the Soviet Army came closer, the German guards began to vacate their posts: 'We were freed by the advancing Russian army who tore down part of the perimeter fence with their tanks.'[13]

Cy returned to England and stayed in the RAF for another year or so. Around this time a special section of the Colonial Office was set up to offer assistance to black air servicemen:

> They were having a lot of hassles as you can imagine, and they needed people to defend them at court martials and other disputes. So that was my job for about a year, which also fitted in with my plans. When I was finally demobbed, I went to study law at Middle Temple and was called to the Bar in 1950. I went on stage the following year.[14]

Cy found that show business offered him more opportunities to earn a living. He began as a calypso singer and then accepted work as an actor. In addition to his regular appearances on BBC television's *Tonight* programme, he played Othello at the Phoenix Theatre in Leicester in 1965. He also provided the voice for Lieutenant Green (aka Seymour Griffiths), the Trinidadian defender of the planet Earth, in the popular 1960s television marionette/science fiction series *Captain Scarlet and the Mysterons*. The casting of Cy was a by-product of his wartime RAF experiences because the creator of the series, Gerry Anderson, had lost his own brother over the Netherlands in the war, and he drew upon Cy's insights to develop one of the first positive black fictional characters in children's television.

In the 1970s, frustrated and disillusioned with the lack of opportunities for black artistes, he co-founded Drum, a London-based black arts centre. He told

Gus John: 'We suffered the indignity of seeing white actors blackening themselves and giving themselves bulbous lips to play black parts, reinforcing the caricature of us as black people, a caricature which casting directors, artistic directors and playwrights themselves refused to allow us to escape.'[15]

During his wartime captivity, Cy began making notes for a memoir which was published as *Blackness and the Dreaming Soul* (2007). In 2008 he assisted in setting up an online archive to trace and commemorate Caribbean aircrew from the Second World War.[16] He also participated in Steven Hatton's *Into the Wind*, a moving documentary film about Bomber Command veterans. He died on 3 February 2010 at the age of 90, but not before learning more about what had happened when his aircraft was shot down over Holland in 1943:

> I was to learn many years later that one of the engines of the Lancaster had gone through the roof of the home of a Dutch farmer killing his wife outright. The incident so disturbed a young boy of the village that he resolved, when he grew up, to trace the entire history of that fatal flight that had traumatised his village. He would discover the name of the Squadron where the bomber had been based in England and all the details of the mission. After a long and arduous investigation, the young Dutchman spectacularly fulfilled his boyhood promise by successfully contacting first the Air Ministry and then the RAF 103 Squadron for details of the mission on the night in question – from the number of bombers from its base at Elsham Wolds in Lincolnshire that had joined in the massive onslaught on the Ruhr, down to the actual plane that had crashed into his village, and the names of the members of its crew. The writer had also contacted each surviving member of the crew, including myself, and compared our versions of events in order to produce an authentic document of our final mission … The most striking part of this chapter of my life story is that, in the midst of a 'Boy's Own' adventure, we find the making and resolution of a personal tragedy in Holland, the formation of a lasting bond between Canadian and West Indian and English and Dutch, forged in the skies over Germany, and a relevant and compelling comment on racial attitudes of the time and how it affected and continues to affect my entire life.[17]

In 2008 the BBC correspondent Kurt Barling persuaded Cy to return for the first time to the village in the Netherlands where he was found. In his obituary of Cy, Barling recalled:

> On that trip he recalled the absurdity of thinking he could escape through Europe to Spain; a black man in occupied Europe had no means of disguise. I wanted to capture the emotions of the Dutch, who revere allied aircrews as their liberators. The farm where he was taken to have a head wound treated still existed. Cy remembered the farmer's pregnant mother; the farmer had been the

unborn baby. As an 11-year-old, one local man, Joost Klootwijk, rushed to the scene of the crash. In later years he was so determined to flesh out that childhood memory and find out what happened to the crew that he spent his early retirement reconstructing the events of Flight W4827 and made contact with Grant. When they finally met during BBC filming, Joost was overcome with emotion several times just being in the presence of a man he had pictured in his mind as a real life hero since he was a boy. The tears flowed freely. I know Grant was humbled by the esteem in which RAF aircrew are held by the Dutch and rather regretted that RAF personnel had not been recognised in this way at home.[18]

Notes

1 Information about other black prisoners of war is difficult to find. In his book *Against Race: Imagining Political Culture Beyond the Color Line* (Harvard University Press, 2000), pp. 303–4, Paul Gilroy mentions Ransford Boi: 'A seaman in the British merchant fleet [who] was captured off the coast of Liberia in December 1939 and transferred to the [Stalag XB] camp at Sandbostel between Bremen and Hanover. He spent two years there before moving to another unnamed internment camp where there were about thirty other black inmates. The regime was relaxed enough for him to have a number of unlikely picaresque adventures.'

2 Jim Pines (ed.), *Black and White in Colour: Black People in British Television since 1936* (BFI Publishing, 1992), pp. 43–4.

3 Ibid.

4 Ibid.

5 Cy Grant, *'A Member of the RAF of Indeterminate Race': WW2 Experiences of a Former RAF Navigator and POW* (Woodfield Publishing, 2006), p. 27.

6 Alec Lom, 'The men of bomber command: the navigator, Cy Grant', *The Telegraph*, 24 October 2008.

7 Ibid.

8 Ibid.

9 Grant, *'A Member of the RAF of Indeterminate Race'*, p. 64.

10 *The Forgotten Volunteers*, BBC Radio 2, 11 November 2000.

11 Pines (ed.), *Black and White in Colour*, p. 44.

12 Lom, *The Telegraph*.

13 Ibid.

14 Pines (ed.), *Black and White in Colour*, p. 44.

15 Gus John, 'Obituary: Cy Grant', *The Guardian*, 18 February 2010.

16 www.caribbeanaircrew-ww2.com.

17 Cy Grant, 'Cy Grant from Guyana', Moving Here (200 years of migration to England) website: www.movinghere.org.uk.

18 Kurt Barling, 'Obituary: Cy Grant – Pioneer for black British actors', *The Independent*, 27 February 2010.

CHAPTER 7

BILLY STRACHAN: A PASSAGE TO ENGLAND

Billy Strachan was raised in a comfortable middle-class Jamaican family. In BBC Radio 4's *The Invisible Force* (16 May 1989) he described his upbringing:

> We'd been brought up to be so British I think of my youth as much more British than the average British child. We sang 'God Save the King' at breakfast. When the news came on in the evening my father always had us all stand to attention. We were so conditioned that we listened to all the broadcasts from this country about the war in Europe, and also it was a desire for adventure. That above all was the thing that drove most of us who wanted to come.

However, Billy knew that if he had asked his father for permission to travel to England, 'he'd have completely squashed the idea. As conservative as he was, he inherently suspected Britain and I knew he wouldn't support the idea.'[1]

Billy also told interviewer Conrad Wood from the Imperial War Museum that to join the RAF would be 'a wonderful opportunity to fly aeroplanes because my dream in life was to have a motor car':

> I had had motor cycles and raced them. I had ridden them on the wall of death. I was an athlete. But the only aeroplanes we had seen in Jamaica were Pan-American sea planes. My idea was to fly an aeroplane. I never worried about death or independence for Jamaica or fascism. Like the majority of people in the Caribbean, and I'm talking about ninety per cent, Britain was home. Our homeland. We were all proud to be British. The Royal Family by its trips and visits around the colonies kept this association with most colonial countries. We in the Caribbean particularly were convinced that we were a distant part of the British Empire. We sang songs, waved Union Jack flags. There was terrific faith in Britain.[2]

William Arthur Watkin Strachan, born in Kingston, Jamaica, in 1921, had only recently left Wolmer's Boys' School in Kingston and taken a job with Jamaica's civil service when he saw the war as an adventure which would permit him to fly aeroplanes. Billy had no idea how difficult this was going to be. He visited the British Army base in Jamaica and told them he wanted to join the RAF:

I had just left school. I had difficulty getting past the guards to speak to someone official, but when I did convince someone that I wanted to join the armed forces, I had a medical, and was passed fully fit because of my athleticism and sporting activities. A friend of mine, a Jamaican white, went with me. We both passed fit. So we then said to the British Army: 'Right. We want to join. Will you send us to England?' We were laughed out: 'You find your own way there!' We thought they would welcome us, two young, healthy volunteers. So how was I going to get out of Jamaica to get to England?[3]

In 1940 Billy sold some of his possessions to pay for his fare to Britain:

I went to the Jamaican Fruit Shipping Company, the major shippers of bananas in those days, and they had a number of boats which were bringing middle-class white people who were fleeing from England and the war to the colonies, including Jamaica, as well as the United States, a safe haven. I was able to per-suade the management that I could be given a passage back to England, and I was asked to pay a reduced fare, from £45 to £15. I didn't even have £15. So I sold my bicycle and my saxophone and with the proceeds I had about £17, paid my £15, and got on a ship, and left Jamaica with about £2 10s. and a small case with one change of clothes. That's how I came to England.[4]

In March 1940 Billy arrived in Bristol: 'I remember the train station. A porter came towards me in his uniform. "Your case, sir," he said and I saluted him. I thought he was a bloody admiral in his uniform. I didn't dare think that he would take my case. "No, sir!" I said.'[5]

Taking the train to Paddington in London Billy attempted to join the RAF by heading straight for the head office of the Air Ministry at a place called Adastral House, which was at the foot of Aldwych. On his arrival he approached a corporal, who Billy thought was the head of the RAF, and was told, in no uncertain terms, to 'piss off!' Billy persisted until a sergeant intervened and informed Billy that he could not join the RAF at the Air Ministry. He would have to go to a recruiting station. The sergeant asked him where he came from and Billy replied, 'Kingston'. The sergeant informed him that there was a recruiting station in Kingston in Surrey, but when Billy explained he had travelled from Kingston, Jamaica, the sergeant didn't know where Jamaica was. A young English RAF pilot overheard this conversation, and said: 'Oh, you're from Jamaica, one of our colonial friends! Welcome. I did geography at University and I've always been impressed with you West Africans. Come in.' Billy later said that, thanks to the pilot's 'supreme igno-rance' and intervention, 'I was dragged in and introduced to a Flight Lieutenant'.

Billy joined the RAF and, after twelve weeks of basic military training, became a wireless operator/air gunner. In 1941 he joined a squadron of Wellington bombers which made nightly raids over heavily defended German industrial cities:

In a squad of fifty I was the only non-white, non-British person. On the first day I am put in the squad, the chap in charge, known as the physical training officer, called out 'Darkie. The black one. You're going to be in charge of the squadron.' It was the first time in my life I had been called darkie. I had never been called darkie in my life before. I was shattered. In Jamaica darkie was a term of contempt. I had conflict in my mind. I was annoyed I was called darkie, but my chest swelled out because I was regarded as a man fit to be promoted to second airman in the RAF![6]

Billy survived thirty operations: 'We were the only crew to finish a tour of operations alive at Waterbeach, a tour being thirty trips. Most of us were young and cocky, and full of our own competence, it didn't worry us at all.'[7] Billy was entitled to a job on the ground but, when asked what he wanted to do, replied at once: 'Retrain as a pilot!' Billy learned so fast that he was allowed to fly solo after only seven hours' training. He loved playing tricks, joyriding, and paying unauthorised visits to friends on airfields all over England. He had several narrow escapes: 'I suppose we had the over-confidence of youth. We never thought it would happen to us. As a crew, we did everything together. At the end of a raid we came back, had parties, checked up to see who were lost and heartlessly said things like "Oh, I'll have his girlfriend, or his bike, if he isn't coming back".'[8]

At Cranwell Billy had his first batman (servant), a man who had been batman to King George VI. Billy described him as 'a real, smooth Jeeves type': 'I was a little coloured boy from the Caribbean and I instinctively called him "Sir". "No, Sir," he hastily corrected, "It is I who call you, 'Sir'".'[9]

Asked how he dealt with racism in the war, Billy replied:

It was there, all right. But my own experience, together with that of most of my colleagues, showed that whenever one [black person] arrived anywhere, he was always welcomed and treated well. When you arrived in England anywhere as a black man you were treated like a teddy bear. You were loved and feted. Two black men, they coped with. It was when three or more came that racism really got sharp, showing this inherent fear and threat that they see of this different animal. I know that some of us fared badly. But I had no problems in that respect.[10]

Billy crashed while performing aerobatics, breaking a hip and damaging his face. He resumed flying as soon as he could, as a bomber pilot. In 1942 Pilot Officer Strachan was famous for his hair-raising but clever way of escaping German fighters: 'The trick was to wait until the enemy was right on your tail and, at the last minute, cut the engine, sending your lumbering Lancaster into a plunging dive, letting the fighter overshoot harmlessly above.'[11]

In 1945 Billy lost his nerve and was reassigned to ground duties as a welfare officer:

It was my last trip and I lost my nerve. I was carrying a 12,000 pound (6,000 kilogram) bomb destined for some German shipping. We were stationed in Lincolnshire and our flight path was over Lincoln Cathedral. It was a foggy night. I asked my engineer, who stood beside me, to make sure we were on course to get over the top of the cathedral tower. He replied: 'We've just passed it.' I looked out and suddenly realised that it was just beyond our wingtips, to the side. This was the last straw. It was sheer luck. I hadn't seen it at all – and I was the pilot! There and then my nerve went. I knew I simply couldn't go on – that this was the end of me as a pilot! I was so shaken I said, 'I can't go on tonight. We must go back.' But you can't land an aeroplane full of petrol and a bomb. You're not allowed. So I had to ask for permission to go to the place in the North Sea where we dropped useless bombs. No allied shipping ever went there. We went off. Dropped the bombs. Jettisoned the petrol. Came back and landed. And then I was sent to a special place in Coventry, a vast country house, but I was only there for forty-eight hours. I talked to a psychiatrist. He said it was tiredness and war weariness.[12]

Billy was demobilised in 1946. He later worked as a legal administrator and, as a political activist, joined the Communist Party and became the secretary of the London branch of the Caribbean Labour Congress, which in the British Caribbean represented the most radical aspect of trade unionism. In 1955 Billy told an interviewer in the Pathé film newsreel *Our Jamaica Problem*: 'Our people from the West Indies have no enmity to any British people. We will be a strength to them. They are ambitious but they will not undercut trade unionists. They will help in the cultural life and co-operate with the British people. They ask for no special privileges or anything more than the British worker.'

Billy died in 1998 and his friend, Marika Sherwood, paid tribute to him in the Black and Asian Studies Association's newsletter: 'Billy suffered all his life from the consequences of his war wounds which became more painful as the years wore on, but he never let this prevent him from carrying on with his writing and his multifarious activities.'[13]

Notes

1   Joshua Levine, *Forgotten Voices of the Blitz and the Battle of Britain* (Ebury Press, 2006), pp. 106–8.

2   William Strachan, interviewed by Conrad Wood for the Imperial War Museum, 26 October 1987. Reference 10042.

3   Ibid.

4   Ibid.

5   Levine, *Forgotten Voices*, p. 107.

6   *The Invisible Force*, BBC Radio 4, 16 May 1989.

7   Ibid.
8   'Caribbean participants in the Second World War', Memorial Gates Trust, www.mgtrust.org.
9   Ibid.
10 Ibid.
11 Ibid.
12 'Caribbean participants in the Second World War' and *The Invisible Force*.
13 Marika Sherwood, 'Billy Strachan (1921–1998)', *Black and Asian Studies Association Newsletter*, No. 22, September 1998, pp. 31–2. See also Peter D. Fraser, 'William Strachan (1921–1998)', *Oxford Dictionary of National Biography* (Oxford University Press, 2004; www.oxforddnb.com).

CHAPTER 8

ULRIC CROSS: A FINE EXAMPLE

In 1941 around 250 Trinidadians travelled to Britain to serve in the RAF. Fifty-two were killed in action and their names are now displayed on a memorial at the Chaguaramas Museum in Port of Spain, Trinidad and Tobago. Ulric Cross is one of those who survived, in spite of flying on eighty bombing missions to Germany and Occupied France. He has been described as the highest-ranking and one of the most distinguished West Indian airmen in the Second World War. He was awarded the Distinguished Flying Cross (DFC) in June 1944 and the Distinguished Service Order (DSO) in November 1944. The League of Coloured Peoples congratulated Ulric in the December 1944 edition of their Newsletter, and informed its readers that they believed he was the first 'coloured' West Indian to receive the DSO.[1] The citation for the DSO reads:

> This officer has set a fine example of keenness and devotion to duty. He has participated in a very large number of sorties, most of which have been against such heavily defended targets as Berlin, Hamburg, Ludwigshaven, and industrial centres in the Ruhr. He is a brave and resolute member of aircraft crew, whose exceptional navigational ability has been an important factor in the successes obtained. His services have been of immense value.[2]

Ulric was born Philip Cross in Port of Spain, Trinidad, in 1917 and decided to volunteer for the RAF after he witnessed the defeat of the British at Dunkirk in 1940; he could see that the Nazis were continuing to gain power across Europe. In 1941, with 250 other Trinidadians, Ulric travelled for twelve days across the Atlantic Ocean to start his training at RAF Cranwell at Sleaford in Lincolnshire. In the BBC Radio 2 documentary *The Forgotten Volunteers*, he recalled:

> We came by boat and we landed at Greenock, in Scotland, in November. It was cold, depressed, and one of the things I shall never forget was getting into RAF transport after getting off the ship. There were a lot of young airmen in this RAF transport and, having lived a gentle life, the first thing I noticed was the language. I have never forgotten it. I had never heard four-letter words used so frequently.

Among the skills he learnt were wireless operation, meteorology, bomb aiming, navigation and Morse code. After he graduated as a pilot officer, Ulric was assigned to Bomber Command and he served as a navigator in 139 (Jamaica) Squadron.[3] Ulric was the only West Indian in 139 Squadron, but it was very cosmopolitan and included Polish, Indian, English, Welsh, Scottish, Scandinavian and Dutch aircrew.

Initially he flew in a very fast, small, ply-board, two-man bomber called the Mosquito:

> We did a lot of low-level daylight bombing. We flew at just fifty feet instead of the normal 25,000 feet. We dropped four 500-pound bombs. You flew in to your target at 50 feet and as you approached it you went up to 1,200 feet. You then did a shallow dive onto the target and released your bombs. The bomb had an 11-second delay, so you shot up to avoid the bomb blast. We went over in formation and we bombed in formation, but we came back independently. I did eight such missions.[4]

The speed of the Mosquito initially allowed it to escape the German anti-aircraft fire, known as 'flak', but the Germans soon discovered this and started shooting down many planes. Ulric mourned the death of one of the pilots who was shot down on his seventh mission. Flying Officer Kenrick Wyville Rawlins of the Royal Air Force Volunteer Reserve was killed in action at the age of 27 on 13 August 1943. He and Ulric had been former pupils of Saint Mary's College, a government-assisted Catholic secondary school in the heart of Port of Spain.

When the RAF realised that 80 per cent of their bombs missed their targets, they established a Pathfinder Force to guide the bombers. Ulric joined them:

> We dropped flares over the target and bombers coming after us would then bomb our flares. There were about a dozen Pathfinders followed by hundreds of bombers. Sometimes when we dropped our flares the Germans would then drop decoy markers fifty miles away. To combat that we were told to drop our bombs at a particular time, with just a ten-second leeway either side. Punctuality was essential to the job. I did eighty operational flights over Germany, including twenty-one to Berlin. We never had guns; we depended for our safety on accurate navigation and speed. You can't be trained not to be afraid but trained to conquer fear. It comes from a belief that what you're doing is right and is worthwhile. All your flight you are busy, busy, busy. The pilot has more time to be afraid than you do. But when the flak starts coming at you and you are 'coned' in a searchlight you feel fear. But your job is to get to the target on time and that is what you are preoccupied with.[5]

Ulric says that one of the biggest dangers was being 'coned' in a searchlight when the German fighters were around:

If you can't get out of the light you watch for fighters. I was once coned for fifteen minutes going to Berlin. The searchlights light up the whole sky. You can't see yourself lit up but you can see other aircraft in cones. They all look silver whatever their actual colour. It's amazing. They really stand out. You can be seen for miles around by fighters and flak. My plane was hit by flak many times.[6]

After enemy flak destroyed one of his plane's two engines, Ulric was almost killed when the plane crash-landed:

We flew home over the whole of Germany on one engine at just 7,000 feet at a reduced speed. It was very dangerous because of fighters. At one stage my pilot told me we might have to bail out. He said, 'Put on your parachute.' I didn't like the idea but we stuck with the plane. We couldn't make it back to our RAF base at Wyton. I had to work out a course to the nearest other RAF base, Swanton Morley, also in East Anglia. When we eventually came in to land, the RAF base wasn't expecting us and we couldn't tell them because we had to maintain radio silence otherwise the Germans would have pinpointed us. There was no flare path on the runway. Instead of circling, we went straight in. We overshot and landed halfway along the runway. We went over the end of the runway and through a hedge. We plunged into a disused quarry. My pilot said, 'Ulric, this is it.' I said, 'Yes, Jack.' We thought we were going to die. We were both rather cool about it. Fortunately the landing speed of the Mosquito was not fast, especially with just one engine. We both hit our heads very badly, but we survived.[7]

In 1943 Ulric made an appearance in the short documentary film *West Indies Calling* with the Jamaican broadcaster Una Marson and Trinidadian welfare officer Learie Constantine. Ulric heard on the radio that the war was over, and he went to Piccadilly Circus in London to join the celebrations:

Everybody was overjoyed and I just didn't feel like taking any part in it. So I went back home. I just felt that a lot of people had been killed. This was not a cause for celebration. The war did not stop people from being killed and a lot of my friends were killed, at least four or five from Trinidad. I was extremely glad the war was over.[8]

In January 1945 the Newsletter of the League of Coloured Peoples noted that Ulric had been appointed the first liaison officer for West Indians in the RAF. They added that the recent award of the DSO to Ulric was 'a joy to every West Indian heart'.

After the war, Ulric qualified as a barrister and worked as a talks producer for BBC radio. He went to Ghana in 1956 when it became independent to work in the Attorney General's office and then went to Cameroon as Attorney General.

Subsequently, he went to Tanzania as a high court judge and dean of the Faculty of Law at the university. In 1974 he returned to Trinidad as a high court judge.

In 1990 Ulric was featured on BBC television in the discussion programme *Hear-Say*. He told the presenter, Jacqui Harper, that he had joined the RAF because he was young, adventurous and idealistic. He said he hated 'the frustrations and the stultifying nature of colonial society, particularly in a very small country', but added that 'the whole idea of being a member of the Royal Air Force was romantic'. Hitler's treatment of the Jews was also 'an important element', but for Ulric the romantic view of the RAF had been with him since his schooldays. He explained that, at the age of 14, he had written his name as 'Flight Lieutenant P.N.U. Cross DFC' in the flyleaves of two of his school books: 'To me that was the height of anybody's ambition, to be a Flight Lieutenant in the Royal Air Force and to get the DFC. Most of my friends thought I was mad.'[9]

Ulric's wartime experiences in the RAF were relatively free of racist attitudes; however, one of his Trinidadian compatriots did not fare so well. Owen Sylvestre, who also joined the RAF in 1941 and eventually received the Distinguished Flying Medal (DFM), was regularly victimised by his CO, who kept calling him to his office to reprimand him for incorrect saluting. Owen Sylvestre gritted his teeth and decided to show the CO and his squadron that he was as good as they were: 'My crew – all whites – respected and trusted me completely.'[10]

Reflecting on his experiences of wartime Britain for Mike and Trevor Phillips' book *Windrush*, Ulric said:

We were treated very well, people were welcoming. One thing is we were in uniform. And the whole atmosphere was very different … People were curious, children would stop you. Almost impossible to walk through a village without children stopping you to ask you the time, and you knew they merely wanted to hear you speak … I was on Mosquitoes, Pathfinder Force, bombing and target marking pathfinders, and I did almost eighty operations. I was lucky … I crash landed I think five or six, seven times … the strange thing is that when you're really young you feel immortal. That may well be a defence mechanism, but you do feel immortal, and you knew that obviously the possibility existed, that every time you got up in an aeroplane and flew over Germany you wouldn't come back. That possibility always existed. But the young feel they will live forever … And I felt I was doing the right thing in trying to stop Hitler. I never felt I was going to the aid of the mother country. Some people did but I would say the majority of us didn't. Reasons differ, but certainly for myself, you're young, this was a tremendous adventure and you were doing it for the right reasons.[11]

Notes

1   League of Coloured Peoples, Newsletter No. 63 (December 1944), p. 63.

2   Edward Scobie, *Black Britannia: A History of Blacks in Britain* (Johnson Publishing, 1972), p. 191.

3   Erica Myers-Davis, *Under One Flag: How Indigenous and Ethnic Peoples of the Commonwealth and British Empire Helped Great Britain Win World War II* (Get Publishing, 2009), pp. 98–9.

4   Sean Douglas, 'World War II Airman Ulric Cross Recalls "The Day I Almost Died"', *Trinidad Express*, 15 November 1999, p. 11.

5   Ibid.

6   Ibid.

7   Ibid.

8   *The Forgotten Volunteers*, BBC Radio 2, 11 November 2000.

9   *Hear-Say*, BBC2, 7 August 1990.

10 Robert N. Murray, *Lest We Forget: The Experiences of World War II West Indian Ex-Service Personnel* (Nottingham West Indian Combined Ex-Services Association/Hansib, 1996), pp. 80–1.

11 Mike Phillips and Trevor Phillips, *Windrush: The Irresistible Rise of Multi-Racial Britain* (HarperCollins, 1998), pp. 27–9.

CHAPTER 9

CONNIE MARK: A FORMIDABLE FORCE

With the fiftieth anniversary of the outbreak of war approaching in 1989, Connie Mark, a former member of the ATS from Jamaica, was hurt that the contribution of West Indians, especially women, was being ignored. When she was interviewed by Jacqui Harper for BBC television's *Hear-Say* in 1990, she said that she had a 'bee in my bonnet' about this absence because 'every time I mentioned that I had been in the army, people would say they didn't know there were any black people in the war'. During the planning of an Age Concern exhibition to commemorate the anniversary, Connie took along some photographs of West Indian ex-servicewomen: 'That caused such a stir. People said, "We never knew there were black ex-servicewomen", and that we even came to England. They are still ignorant.'[1]

So Connie applied to the Greater London Arts and they gave her a grant; she was able to find some photographs in the Imperial War Museum, as well as borrow a few from ex-servicewomen from across the West Indies, and she put together an exhibition for the 1989 fiftieth anniversary celebrations. When asked by Jacqui Harper what the reaction was to her exhibition, Connie replied: 'Shock. But I'm very glad that I stood my ground and I've done it and if I die tomorrow I have achieved what I wanted to have done.'

After war was declared in 1939, Connie remembered 'a mood of fear in Jamaica'. She said the English 'put the fear of God in us':

> We were definitely positively told that the Germans wanted us because we were a stepping stone to the coast of America. So we were on our tenterhooks all the time. Like England, Jamaica is an island. We depended on boats bringing things in. So if you are short of oil because the boat coming in was torpedoed, then the whole bloody island has no oil.[2]

Connie also remembered the English officers who would 'go into all the little corners of Jamaica and they would beg, literally beg you to come and fight for England'.[3]

Connie said that most of the Jamaican men who were recruited came from the countryside and they had never left home. So it came as a shock when they found themselves packed four to a bunk on a troopship: 'It was like pushing animals together because they really had the ships all cramped to make sure they got as many as they could to fight for England.'[4] Connie was made aware of the dangers that surrounded Jamaica and the other islands of the Caribbean. Ships were vulnerable to being torpedoed by the German U-boats (an abbreviation of *Unterseeboot*: undersea boat or submarine) that patrolled the Caribbean seas: 'Guyana had a lot of gold and the Germans wanted to get it, and they also wanted oil from Trinidad, so there was a lot of submarines watching the island. It was very frightening.'[5] Connie remembered the air-raid wardens who went around the towns and villages in Jamaica: 'If by chance you had a speck of light showing from your house, you'd be arrested and fined.'[6]

Connie was born Constance MacDonald in Rollington Town, Kingston, Jamaica, in 1923. Her paternal grandfather was a white Scotsman; her maternal grandfather was an indentured labourer from Calcutta. Her maternal grandmother was half-Lebanese, while her paternal grandmother was Jamaican. Two of her uncles had been killed in the Boer war and her father taught in a school for the children of British Army personnel. Connie saw herself as British, and patriotic: 'England was our mother country. We were brought up to respect the Royal Family. I used to collect pictures of Princess Margaret and Princess Elizabeth. I adored them.'[7]

Connie was just 19 years old in 1943 when she joined the British Army in Jamaica. Unlike other women from the Caribbean islands who joined up, Connie served her time in Jamaica: 'I was going to take my exams in bookkeeping when my teacher came and said that they needed an expert and she said I was the best person.'[8] Connie was taken by the teacher to Up Park Camp, which was the military headquarters on South Camp Road in Kingston. Connie served in the ATS, the women's branch of the British Army, for ten years. She worked as a medical secretary at the British Military Hospital in Kingston and her duties included typing up the medical reports of those who had been injured in battle. Connie found herself documenting the terrible injuries men had sustained in bombings and combat:

I volunteered myself as a Medical Secretary and I was secretary to the Assistant Director of Medical Services. Having to type the medical reports really brought home the reality of war. I was still in my formative years. When you are in the army you are on 24 hours duty. You know nothing about off duty, so I used to have my uniform hung up all the while. My mother died so I lived with my aunt and anywhere I was going my aunt had to know where I was because if a troop ship was coming in at 2am in the morning then the Military Police would come to my home, knock on the door and, in five minutes flat, I had to be dressed to go out. If I wasn't there my aunt would have to say she's gone to a night club here and there. The Military Police would come to get me wherever I was and I had to be down at that troop ship. And that's really when the reality of war came home to me because you saw men leaving hale and hearty and you see them coming back on stretchers, you see them coming back in wheelchairs, some blind.[9]

If Jamaicans wanted to find out if any of their loved ones had gone missing or had been killed in action, they went to Kingston Town: 'At a place they call Parade there were two lists – a list of men reported missing and a list of men reported dead. And that list would go on and on – sometimes you'd go and you'd see the name of your cousin; you'd go back a few days later and see your friend's brother reported dead.'[10]

At Up Park Camp there was a POW camp and when war was declared all the German and Italian seamen working on merchant ships in the area were taken off and taken to the internment camp in Up Park Camp:

I worked at the hospital, and if they were sick they had to come up there for treatment. And we had a special corps that guarded them. They were called the 'Pioneer Corps'. It's quite interesting because we had a lot of Germans in Jamaica because about 150 years ago a whole village in Germany emigrated to Jamaica, around Seaford Town and St Elizabeth. Now I think back about it, most of the people they had guarding them were German-Jamaicans from Seaford Town … The Germans and Italians have a lot of talent, so they used to make a lot of leather goods, and maybe twice a year they'd sell their wares that they made. And I remember I bought a lovely leather writing case. We used to buy things that they made. And another man was very proficient: he made doll's furniture. He must have been a carpenter or something in Germany. I remember I bought a whole drawing room and bedroom suite for my niece made by the German internee.[11]

Connie remembered the fights that broke out, especially when the Irish Fusiliers arrived in Jamaica:

They all got drunk and they used to fight! They fought the Jamaicans they met in bars. And of course when they're coming to go to camp the Jamaicans waylaid them. So sometimes a whole road had to be put out of bounds because of fighting white soldiers. And we had the Brockville Rifles from Canada. And they could fight! They were always fighting! But a lot of it was prejudices, you see. They are white and they come to Jamaica and they just couldn't handle it. They just felt that they was kings, that, 'I can do anything and go anywhere.' And of course Jamaican soldiers – no, not necessarily soldiers but Jamaicans, whether soldiers or not – took exceptions to it. So they started some nice good fight. Fortunately with the Americans it wasn't so bad because the Americans wasn't in Kingston. They were in St Catherine, in another parish. Their base was actually in a place called Sandy Gully. We did not have that much to do with them. But everyone wanted to go and work on the American base because the pay was good.[12]

Food shortages were common throughout the war and Connie said that, when rice and peas were rationed, asking a Jamaican not to eat them on a Sunday was considered a crime!

And I remember once we were running very, very short. Everyone loves rice in Jamaica, most people. And a ship that was coming was torpedoed near Guyana. And instead of having rice we were having spaghetti and things like that. And oil! We haven't got oil in Jamaica, and if a ship was torpedoed that's it, we wouldn't have any oil.[13]

Eventually, Connie rose to the rank of corporal:

It was quite an achievement to even reach the rank of Corporal. When you are a Lance Corporal, army regulations state that once one is promoted to Corporal you are entitled to tuppence per day. I applied for my tuppence a day and was turned down by the War Office. When I asked why, I was told the Jamaican ATS were not entitled to this. I was in a British regiment attached to the Royal Army Medical Corps but I was still not entitled. That was my first experience of racial discrimination. The Queen still owes me eight years of tuppence a day! That may not sound a lot now, but in those days it added up. So I have had my little prejudices thrown at me.[14]

Connie remembered VE Day as a marvellous time:

Everybody was happy 'cause as far as we were concerned, the war was finished. Everybody was happy. Everybody just jumped up and down; the war was over, and it meant that no more of our people would be killed. We had parties, and everybody took it as an excuse to have a party, a drink up, and get stone-blind drunk. I didn't used to drink in those days; I just went to all the parties that there were. Yeah, you were glad that the war was over, and people weren't going to die. You didn't have troop ships coming in with people sick, or blinded, or with missing limbs.[15]

When the war ended, Connie's commander put her up for the British Empire Medal (BEM), but she did not receive it. She believed she was overlooked because she refused to clean the houses of the English ATS officers. However, in 1992 she did finally receive the BEM, nearly forty years after she had left Jamaica and settled in London. When Connie arrived in London in 1954, she said:

There were very few people who didn't have a story of having lost someone or knew someone who lost someone, or telling you of streets that had been bombed ... the war was still very much part of what was happening in Britain, and people were living in prefabs, and that was quite strange. You couldn't understand why they were living in what we saw as huts. I get very annoyed that people don't want to accept and remain ignorant of the fact of how the West Indies were involved in the war and how we were brought up to love the King, love the Queen, to love England and to respect England. Then when you come here after the war, what do you see? You see a sign saying 'No Blacks, no Irish, no dogs, no children'. That hurt, that really used to hurt.[16]

When Connie joined the West Indian ex-Servicemen's Association she raised the profile of the contribution women had made to the British war effort, and persuaded the organisation to extend its name to the West Indian ex-Servicemen and Women's Association. Health permitting, she regularly marched in the annual Remembrance Day parade at the Cenotaph. Inspired by the Jamaican doctress Mary Seacole (1805–81), a heroine of the Crimean war, Connie was instrumental in founding the Friends of Mary Seacole organisation, which has since become the Mary Seacole Memorial Association. In 2001 Connie was awarded the MBE.

When she died in 2007, her obituarist, Margaret Busby, described her as a champion of Caribbean culture and 'a formidable force within the black community. She was much in demand for her poetry and storytelling events, using oral history to address the young.'[17] In 2008 Connie was posthumously honoured with a blue plaque by the Nubian Jak Community Trust, in association with Care UK and Hammersmith and Fulham Council. It was unveiled by Councillor Andrew Johnson, the Mayor of Hammersmith and Fulham, at Connie's former home, Mary Seacole House, in Invermead Close, Hammersmith.[18]

Notes

1   Ben Bousquet and Colin Douglas, *West Indian Women at War: British Racism in World War II* (Lawrence and Wishart, 1991), p. 144.

2   Christopher Somerville, *Our War: How the British Commonwealth Fought the Second World War* (Weidenfeld and Nicolson, 1998), pp. 173–4.

3   Ethnic Communities Oral History Project, *The Motherland Calls: African Caribbean Experiences* (Hammersmith and Fulham Community History Series, No. 4/ECOHP, 1989), p. 1.

4   Ibid., p. 1.

5   Angelina Osborne and Arthur Torrington, *We Served: The Untold Story of the West Indian Contribution to World War II* (Krik Krak Publishing, 2005), p. 17.

6   Oliver Marshall, *The Caribbean at War: British West Indians in World War II* (The North Kensington Archive, 1992), p. 4.

7   *We Served*, p. 17.

8   Ibid., p. 18.

9   Stephen Bourne and Sav Kyriacou (eds), *A Ship and a Prayer* (ECOHP, 1999), p. 24.

10 *We Served*, p. 17.

11 *The Caribbean at War*, p. 21.

12 Ibid., p. 19.

13 Ibid., p. 14.

14 Ibid., p. 24.

15 *We Served*, p. 19.

16 Mike Phillips and Trevor Phillips, *Windrush: The Irresistible Rise of Multi-Racial Britain* (HarperCollins, 1998), pp. 126–7.

17 Margaret Busby, 'Obituary: Connie Mark', *The Guardian*, 16 June 2007.

18 Jon Weisgard, 'Campaigner Connie Mark honoured in blue plaque tribute', *Hammersmith and Fulham News*, 1 July 2008, p. 4.

CHAPTER 10

SAM KING: RAF TO WINDRUSH

In 1944, when Sam King read a newspaper appeal for volunteers for the RAF, the young Jamaican asked his mother for advice. She said: 'My son, the mother country is at war. Go. And if you survive, you will not regret it.'[1] Sam later learned that his mother wept every time she heard that a ship had been torpedoed and sunk. She believed that her son could be among those who were lost forever. Sam later reflected: 'I don't think the British Empire was perfect, but it was better than Nazi Germany.'[2]

Sam King was born in 1926 in Portland, Jamaica, between Priestman's River and Castle River, half a mile from the Caribbean sea: 'I spent a lot of my youth in the waters, therefore I should have joined the Royal Navy if they would have me, but when the war was on the Royal Air Force took me and I think I did my little bit.'[3] Sam came from a farming background and, being the eldest son, was expected to follow in his father's footsteps and become a farmer, but Sam had other ideas. He said he felt 'doomed' to be a farmer, so when he saw an advertisement in the *Daily Gleaner* in 1944, asking for men to join the RAF, he seized the opportunity to leave home and support the war effort:

> There were about three hundred of us, eagerly awaiting the selection procedure. We were given two sets of written tests. Having taken the first … only those whose names were called out could go on to the second test. My heart was pounding and I was apparently temporarily deaf because someone nudged me and said, 'Answer to your name, man.'[4]

Sam passed the second test and travelled to Kingston where he and the other volunteers were escorted to an army camp to undergo a month of intensive training before making the journey to England. They left the camp in October 1944 on the SS *Cuba*.

Sam arrived in Clyde, near Glasgow in Scotland, in November 1944 and to cope with the bitter cold weather he was given a heavy overcoat. Sam's father had been to America and warned his son about winter:

I was shocked when I came to England … it was winter. I came off the troop train and I stepped into about three inches of snow. And it remained on the ground for about one month. It was shocking.[5]

Sam journeyed on a troopship from Clyde to Filey in Yorkshire where he was to undertake training, 'and then something happened near Christmas':

The German Panzers burst out in the Ardennes: the Battle of the Bulge. And for a month or so we weren't looking like we were winning the war, we're looking like we're just holding on. The Americans woke up one morning and found that Panzers were running through them like knife goes through butter. The weather was so bad for three weeks that the aircrafts could not take off. Once the air was clear, we in the air force were working night and day to do what we can to get the aircrafts flying.[6]

Meanwhile, Sam continued to experience his first winter at the Filey barracks:

I don't know why nobody had fire but these billets didn't have. And we just came from the colonies, it was hard. Some mornings when we got up we take our bayonets and cut the ice to get out the door. And I will agree they gave us an extra blanket because we complained. The attitude they had is either you survive or that we get another man from the colonies.[7]

On one occasion, Sam had an encounter with a corporal who had just returned from a posting in South Africa:

Some people were prejudiced. I had an incident in the RAF where a Corporal who was in South Africa came back and saw me in the middle of the room, and said, 'There's a black man there, he can't stay in here.' A friend of mine, who is still a friend of mine after forty-four years, said, 'What rubbish you talking about.' The Corporal said, 'In South Africa black people don't stay in the same room.' My friend said, 'This is not South Africa. This is England, and he came here to fight.'[8]

After Filey, Sam was sent to work at RAF Hawkinge near Folkestone. On the journey from Filey to Hawkinge, Sam stopped off in London, but he wasn't impressed:

It was black, and it was bombed. Just wilderness. The trains were running because if they bombed the tracks, tomorrow morning they repair them. It was terrible. But I had the privilege of flying over Germany a month after the war and they might have given us bad, but I would say there was not a cricket pitch length in Germany that we didn't bomb. I don't think they'll start another war in my lifetime.[9]

On VE Day Sam was at his hangar repairing an aircraft:

> At eleven o'clock in the day the tannoy sounded 'Attention! This is VE Day. The Germans have surrendered and we can have the remainder of the day off but we must remember that there is a war on in Asia so tomorrow we must be back on parade and repairing aircraft.' With my best blue on, I caught the bus and went into Weston-Super-Mare. Everything has stopped. It was different. The birds were singing. I got off the bus and I was on the right-hand side of the road, passing the George and Dragon. A lady rushed out: 'Come along! You must have a drink.' She pulled me in the pub and said 'Bring rum for this airman, he's from Jamaica.' I said, 'I'm very sorry. I do not drink rum.' She said, 'How can you not drink rum? You've got Jamaica on your shoulder!' She brought the rum and I had to drink the rum. She gave me a hard time, but everybody was happy. It was VE Day. There'll be no more bombing. No more killing. And especially for the women whose loved ones were coming home. It was good to be alive and I was alive.[10]

After the war, Sam planned to stay in England and continue serving with the RAF: 'But they said if you are from the colonies you have to go back. I wanted to study because I realised I didn't know enough. I read [George Bernard] Shaw and all that in the library when I was here and I realised I was a peasant mentally and I wanted to stay.'[11]

Sam remained in the RAF until he was demobbed in 1947, and then he returned to Jamaica. However, while he had been away a hurricane had destroyed much of the farm land. In addition to servicemen like Sam, Jamaicans who had been working on the Panama Canal were sent home, as were those who had gone to America to work on farms and in war factories:

> I, being the eldest son, should have been a farmer but when I returned it was shocking. 30,000 of us were thrown back without any planning and I decided that my children would not grow up in a colony because we had no control over education, welfare, health and things you produce. They were decided in London markets. So I had no intention of planting bananas for them at their price. I would rather come to London and work on their terms.[12]

In 1948 Sam returned to England as one of the passengers on the SS *Empire Windrush*. He rejoined the RAF on entering Britain and served until 1953, after which he worked for the Post Office. In 1950 he and his brother became the second black family in the London Borough of Southwark to buy their own home. In the 1950s Sam became involved in his local community and joined the Brixton-based *West Indian Gazette* as its circulation manager. It was this monthly newspaper that spearheaded the origination of the cultural event that celebrated Britain's Caribbean communities, which has since grown to become the world-renowned Notting Hill Carnival. Sam served as a Labour councillor between 1982 and 1986. Although there were other black councillors in Southwark at the time, Sam was the first to become Mayor of Southwark in 1983. In 1998 Sam received an MBE from the Queen for his outstanding services to the community and in 2010 he was honoured with a Southwark Blue Plaque.

Notes

1   Angelina Osborne and Arthur Torrington, *We Served: The Untold Story of the West Indian Contribution to World War II* (Krik Krak Publishing, 2005), p. 13.

2   Stephen Bourne, *Speak of Me As I Am: The Black Presence in Southwark Since 1600* (Southwark Council, 2005), p. 64.

3   *The Invisible Force*, BBC Radio 4, 16 May 1989.

4   Sam King, *Climbing Up the Rough Side of the Mountain* (Minerva Press, 1998), pp. 41–42.

5   Mike Phillips and Trevor Phillips, *Windrush: The Irresistible Rise of Multi-Racial Britain* (HarperCollins, 1998), p. 41.

6   Rory O'Connell's 1993 interview with Sam King, available on the Museum of London's London Voices website: www.museumoflondon.org.uk.

7   Ibid.

8   *The Invisible Force*.

9   Rory O'Connell interview.

10 *The Invisible Force*.

11 Rory O'Connell interview.

12 Jon Surtees, 'Start of a long voyage', *Southwark News*, 20 October 2005, p. 22.

CHAPTER 11

NORMA BEST & NADIA CATTOUSE: LEST WE FORGET

Before the war the majority of white Britons had not come into contact with black women and, if the War Office had had their way, the situation would have stayed the same. For example, on 25 October 1941 Miss L. Curtis, a black Bermudan, applied to join the ATS and was provisionally accepted by the War Office. When it was discovered that she was black, Miss Curtis was informed that there was no suitable vacancy. Joanne Buggins, in an excellent article published in the *Imperial War Museum Review*, says:

> The Governor of Bermuda warned that this rejection would have a most demoralising effect locally, and the Colonial Office was adamant that whatever might happen on the general issue it was quite indefensible that the Department should go back on a definite commitment to Miss Curtis … Only when the Secretary of State for the Colonies, Colonel Oliver Stanley, intervened was this matter settled.[1]

However, it took time for the matter to be settled. In 1943 West Indian women were finally encouraged to join the ATS and some of the women were so keen to come to the mother country and support the war effort that they paid their own passage. The recruits began to arrive in Britain in October 1943. Historian Ben Bousquet said: '381 women actually paid their way across to fight for King and country. They were nice, middle-class black women who wouldn't have done anything anyway other than stay at home. So the war was a form of elevation, a release.'[2]

In 1944 Norma Best joined the ATS in British Honduras, which became known as Belize on its independence in 1981. She was one of those 'nice, middle-class black women' seeking adventure. In 2010, when she was interviewed by a group of students from the Alexander Park Secondary School in Haringey for Patrick Vernon's documentary *Speaking Out and Standing Firm*, Norma explained: 'I volunteered because I wanted to travel and we didn't have many opportunities to travel in those days. And that was the only opportunity so I thought I was going to have it. So I applied and I was accepted.' When the teenagers enquired about her army service and racism, Norma replied:

Serving in the armed forces was wonderful. It was the best experience I've ever had. We were treated well. Our officers looked after us like our mothers. Every step I made in the army was fantastic. I didn't experience any racism because at that time all the people in England wanted to win the war, so colour didn't come into it. We were all fighting for the same thing, to win the war. The English people opened their homes to us, we were invited out for dinners, teas, no problems at all. But I think there were problems with the American forces, but it didn't hinder us.

Norma followed Nadia Cattouse, another Honduran, who had volunteered to join the ATS in 1943. Sixty years later, in 2003, the Windrush Foundation honoured Nadia and a number of other organisations and individuals who had provided an outstanding service to Britain's black community. For their Lifetime Achievement Award for Contribution to the Arts, the Foundation selected Nadia for her distinguished career as an actress and folk singer. However, when Nadia arrived in Britain in 1944, it was not to pursue a career on the stage, but to support the war effort.

Nadia was born in British Honduras where, she said: 'There were some books called Royal Readers and these books taught you all about England but nothing about your own country.'[3] During the war Nadia volunteered for the ATS: 'When the war began the men started to go. I had an uncle in a forestry unit in Scotland, and cousins in the RAF. Eventually they started asking for women volunteers and in 1943 I heard this on the local radio news. I was so eager I jumped on my bike straight away to get to Drill Hall.'[4]

Nadia was signed up and soon joined five other West Indian volunteers to travel to Britain, but they had a lot of travelling to do before they reached their destination. Their first stop – in November 1943 – was Jamaica, where they had initial training, and then they journeyed to Miami in Florida, before passing through Washington D.C. and sailing from New York to Gourock in Scotland. Nadia says she doesn't know why Scotland loomed so large in her mind:

I just knew I was heading for Scotland. I think it was because the colony and the settlement of British Honduras [was] peopled by Scottish-British far more than by the English-British, especially in the early days. Also, the British Honduran Forestry Unit were already in place in Scotland and I had an uncle, Carlton Fairweather, among them.[5]

Nadia Cattouse was in the first group of six women to be recruited in British Honduras. Among the recruits in the second group of six was her friend, Norma Best. Norma and her group took a similar route to Nadia, travelling first to Jamaica where they had their initial training, then on to New Orleans where they received their uniforms, and then to New York where they departed on the RMS *Queen Mary* to Britain.

Norma grew up in Belize City and Spanish Honduras and had 'a lovely childhood. It was a beautiful, perfect country. Safe. Our doors were open. It was a very *British* country.'[6] British Honduras was a colony ruled by England and its people were very loyal. Norma says: 'Changes happened after the war but, when I was growing up, nobody questioned our loyalty to Britain, and there was no resentment of the British.'[7] Norma enjoyed school and dreamed of adventure: 'I used to sit in school and just dream. We had to study the geography of England and I dreamed of these places. I thought I would love to go there.'[8]

Norma did not believe she would ever get to England and at home she wanted to become an actress, but there were no opportunities for this particular dream. In fact, Norma discovered that her only career choices were the civil service, nursing, working in a store, or joining her family in education. She chose the latter and began work in a school. The war changed everything and enabled Norma to fulfil her dreams: 'I was looking for adventure. I had always wanted to travel as a little girl, and this was the opportunity. A few of my relatives and friends said that London was cold and that I might not be able to withstand the weather, but I was determined to go.'[9] Norma's father had served in Egypt in the First World War, having joined the army at the same age as Norma, but she hadn't known about this until she told him of her plans to join the ATS. He told his daughter to 'go for it', while her grandmother called her a 'crazy girl'.

In June 1944 Norma left home for Jamaica 'to become acclimatised':

Jamaica had a base in the mountains which were cold and England was cold. I reported to Kingston six weeks later and then travelled to New Orleans. The British were well in command. They were aware of the racial segregation that existed in America and they made sure we were treated well. They were nice to us in the hotel where we stayed, and we were taken on sight-seeing trips. The same thing happened in New York. People were curious when they saw us in uniform and wanted to know where we came from.[10]

Norma arrived in Scotland in August 1944 and a train took her to London where she was allowed to do some sightseeing before going to Guildford for six weeks of training. On her arrival, she discovered that she knew more about Britain than some of the British. She put that down to her very English education. She was also surprised by the accents: 'I thought everyone would speak proper English! So I was stunned when I heard the Scottish accent, or the Cockney accent.'[11] In 2010 she told the students from Alexander Park Secondary School: 'The training was tough but we did it. We used to get up to mischief. Sometimes we used to take it in turns to hide, not go on parade, because we used to wear shorts for sports in the snow. But it was all done with love.'

Norma's ambition was to be a driver, as her father had been during the First World War, but she could not cope with the weather. Instead, she undertook administrative work, serving in Preston and later Derby. Norma remembers her time serving in the ATS: 'You had to be in at certain times. You had to do certain jobs at certain times and when you went out you had to be on your best behaviour because you're wearing that uniform and whatever you do will reflect on others. The training I received strengthened me in character. But what was in me remained there.'

In London Norma socialised with her colleagues: 'We had a centre in Piccadilly, the Nuffield Centre, where *all* personnel from all different ranks met. Everybody just got on together. You were just wearing different uniforms. We were all friends.'[12] Norma was in London in May 1945 for VE Day and took part in the end-of-war celebrations on the Embankment. She later reflected: 'I think the spirit of the war was that we were all fighting to win. All we could think about is to get in there, do a good job, let's get it over and done with. Colour didn't come into it.'[13] After the war, Norma studied to become a primary school teacher at Durham University and, after marrying and having a family, she worked as a teacher and headmistress from 1961–88.

Notes

1 Joanne Buggins, 'West Indians in Britain during the Second World War: a short history drawing on Colonial Office papers', *Imperial War Museum Review No. 5* (Imperial War Museum, 1990), pp. 93–4. For more information about Miss L. Curtis, see Ben Bousquet and Colin Douglas' *West Indian Women at War: British Racism in World War II* (Lawrence and Wishart, 1991), pp. 97–105.

2 *The Forgotten Volunteers*, BBC Radio 2, 11 November 2000.

3 Nadia Cattouse, *Lest We Forget*, Channel 4, 8 November 1990.

4 Nadia Cattouse, interview with Stephen Bourne, London, 8 August 1989.

5 Cattouse, *Lest We Forget*.

6 Norma Best, interviewed by Toby Brooks for the Imperial War Museum, 11 October 2007. Reference 30492.

7 Ibid.

8 *Birthrights*, BBC2, 5 July 1993.

9 Angelina Osborne and Arthur Torrington, *We Served: The Untold Story of the West Indian Contribution to World War II* (Krik Krak Publishing, 2005), p. 9.

10 Interview by Toby Brooks for the Imperial War Museum.

11 Ibid.

12 *Birthrights*.

13 Ibid.

CHAPTER 12

EDDIE MARTIN NOBLE
& *A CHARMED LIFE*

In 2009 the filmmaker Patrick Vernon premiered his documentary *A Charmed Life*. It told the story of Eddie Martin Noble, a Jamaican who joined the RAF during the Second World War. When Patrick screened *A Charmed Life* at the BFI Southbank, he wrote in *The Guardian*:

> Noble felt very strongly about the lack of acknowledgement of the West Indian contribution to the war and was very critical of Winston Churchill, who he believed did not value or respect the contribution that black servicemen made to the war effort, and who initially tried to block attempts by people from the Caribbean to volunteer.[1]

Patrick was very conscious of the lack of recognition for the West Indians who supported Britain during its hour of need, and his friendship with Eddie led to the making of *A Charmed Life* which enabled the war veteran to express his views. Patrick said in *The Voice*:

> My documentary, *A Charmed Life*, explores Eddie's perspectives and values of inspiring young people and gives a historical perspective on the issues around colonisation of the Caribbean, the colour bar and racial inequality in post-war Britain. One of the key messages that I hope the film can promote is that people like Eddie and other elders are our true mentors, not just footballers, hip hop stars or politicians and minor celebrities. I think it is essential that we record this history for posterity's sake. We have no excuses, as we have the technology – mobile phones, camcorders, Dictaphones and even tape recorders to interview elders from the community. Otherwise, as people born between 1910–1930 will probably have passed away, the next Windrush celebrations in 2018 will be an empty and hollow affair.[2]

Eddie Noble was born in Kingston, Jamaica, in 1917 and by the middle of 1941 he was travelling the island as a sales representative. He continued with this until joining the RAF in 1943. He later recalled in his autobiography: 'From the moment I saw the film *In Which We Serve*, I had made up my mind that no self-respecting able-bodied young man could honourably remain at home when the fate of the world was literally at stake in Europe.'[3]

Noel Coward's patriotic film, *In Which We Serve* (1942), inspired Eddie to join up and he volunteered for the RAF. In Patrick Vernon's film *A Charmed Life*, he said: 'Although I had great respect for the fighting spirit of the British people, I had no time for the bigoted colonial representative in Jamaica.' At the start of the war there was no recruitment in the West Indies for the war effort:

> After I came to England I found that the reason for this is that the Prime Minister, Winston Churchill, objected to black men serving alongside white men on equal terms. But a number of English businessmen in the West Indies wanted to make a contribution to the war effort and they decided they would pay for young men to come to England to volunteer for the air force. The experiment was such a success that the colonial governors in the West Indies brought pressure to bear on the Colonial Office. So Churchill and the government in England was forced to change their attitude and they started recruitment in the West Indies but it had to be voluntary recruitment. And I volunteered.[4]

Eddie acknowledged that Churchill was 'a great war leader'. He believed that, without his leadership, the British people would have lost the war: 'But, to put it bluntly, he was a bastard. As soon as the war ended they threw him out, and let a Labour government in, so that should tell you something.'[5]

Eddie felt that he was treated exactly the same as any other airman, except when he went out with white women. Then he faced objections from white servicemen. However, in *A Charmed Life* he referred to the problems faced by West Indian recruits when they tried for promotion:

> By the end of the war there were 10,000 of us in the RAF, but 99.9% of us never went beyond the rank of Sergeant. The Air Ministry would not admit it. A [white] LAC [leading aircraftman] was working under me. I was a Corporal then and I trained him. And we both sat for an examination that would have moved us to officer cadets. He passed. I failed. I trained him. I know my colour was the reason but no one would admit it.[6]

While on a month's leave, Eddie returned home to Jamaica and found himself the centre of attention. He accepted an invitation to a cocktail party held in his honour, but the sponsors of the party included a member of the white colonial family who had caused his expulsion from an all-white college before the war: 'I waited until they introduced me and when I replied to the introduction I told them who I was, told them what to do with their drinks, and walked out. I know it was rude but, even now, after all these years, that bit of rudeness has given me more satisfaction than almost anything else I've done in my whole life!'[7]

1 The author at the Imperial War Museum, London, 10 March 2007 for his illustrated talk 'We Also Served: Black Women in Wartime Britain, 1939–45' during International Women's Week. *Courtesy of Andrew Warrington*

2 Ros Howells and some Second World War veterans, including Laurent Phillpot, Sam King, Allan Wilmot, Connie Mark and Lilian Bader, outside the Imperial War Museum, London, in 2004. *Courtesy of Georgina Cook/South London Press*

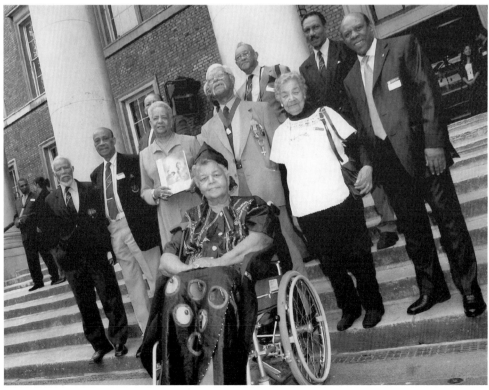

3 Colonel Charles Arundel 'Joe' Moody.
Courtesy of the Moody family

4 Lilian Bader. *Courtesy of the
Imperial War Museum. Ref. HU 53753*

5 Ramsay and Lilian Bader cutting a cake to celebrate their wedding in 1943. They met while he was a tank driver with the Essex Yeomanry and she was serving in the WAAF. *Courtesy of Lilian Bader*

6 Reginald Foresythe. *Author's collection*

7 Sergeant Leslie Thompson on the anti-aircraft battery, Portsmouth, 1943. *Courtesy of Jeffrey Green*

8 Cy Grant, *Into the Wind* (2009). *Courtesy of Steven Hatton/www.intothewind.co.uk*

9 Flight Lieutenant Ulric Cross DSO, DFC, pictured after receiving his decorations at Buckingham Palace on 27 July 1945. *Courtesy of the Imperial War Museum. Ref. HU 58315*

10 Ulric Cross, *Into the Wind* (2009). *Courtesy of Steven Hatton/www.intothewind.co.uk*

11 A group of West Indian ATS recruits
recently arrived at their training camp,
November 1943. *Courtesy of the Imperial War
Museum. Ref. CP 13937D*

12 Sam King at the Imperial War Museum,
London, in 2004. *Courtesy of Georgina Cook/
South London Press*

13 Nadia Cattouse. *Courtesy of Nadia Cattouse*

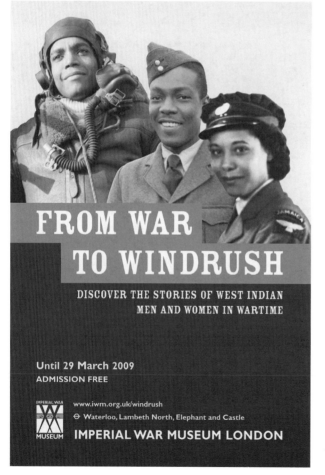

FROM WAR TO WINDRUSH

DISCOVER THE STORIES OF WEST INDIAN
MEN AND WOMEN IN WARTIME

Until 29 March 2009
ADMISSION FREE

www.iwm.org.uk/windrush
Waterloo, Lambeth North, Elephant and Castle

IMPERIAL WAR MUSEUM LONDON

14 From War to Windrush exhibition poster from 2008–09. *Courtesy of the Imperial War Museum*

15 Trinidadian accountant
Jellicoe Scoon recently arrived
in England as an RAF recruit,
in Parliament Square, 26 March
1942. *Courtesy of the Imperial War
Museum. Ref. CH 5213*

16 Sergeant Lincoln Lynch
from Jamaica volunteered for
service in the RAF in 1942.
He completed his training
in Canada and won the Air
Gunner's Trophy in 1943 and
1944. *Courtesy of the Imperial War
Museum. Ref. CH 12263*

17 West Indian RAF ground crew, somewhere in England. *Courtesy of the Black Cultural Archives. Ref. PHOTOS/3*

18 Flight Sergeant Victor Tucker from Jamaica, serving with 129 Squadron, was killed in action on 4 May 1942. *Courtesy of the Imperial War Museum. Ref. CH 5312*

19 James Hyde, a fighter pilot from Trinidad serving with 132 Squadron, is pictured in 1944 by a Supermarine Spitfire with 'Dingo', the squadron commander's pet dog. He was killed in action on 25 September 1944. *Courtesy of the Imperial War Museum. Ref. CH 11978*

W/O J. Hyde ReportedKilled In Operations

W/O HYDE

Warrant Officer James Joseph Hyde, of the Royal Air Force, who was recently reported missing believed killed, lost his life as a result of air operations on September 25.

His father, Mr. J. Hyde, of Santa Cruz, San Juan, has received a letter from the Air Ministry expressing the profound sympathy of the Air Council in his bereavement.

The letter states that Warrant Officer Hyde was killed instantly when his aircraft crashed on September 25 at Elst, near Arnhem, Holland, and was buried by the infantry at the scene of the crash.

20 Newspaper excerpt reporting James Hyde's death.

21 Askaris (East African soldiers) being trained for the war in Burma. *Courtesy of the Imperial War Museum. Ref. K 7686*

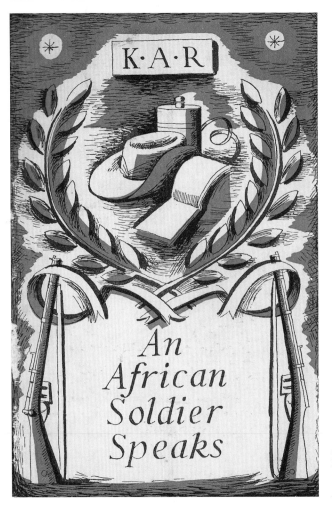

22 Cover of Robert Kakembo's *An African Soldier Speaks* (1946). *Author's collection*

23 Pilot Officer Peter Thomas of Nigeria, the first African to be granted a commission in the RAF. *Courtesy of the Imperial War Museum. Ref. CH 7167*

24 Pilot Officer John Smythe of Sierra Leone, a newly qualified navigator, photographed while undergoing training in Buckinghamshire in 1943. *Courtesy of the Imperial War Museum. Ref. CH 10739*

25 Pilot Officer John Smythe being shown how to use the sextant by an instructor in 1943. *Courtesy of the Imperial War Museum. Ref. CH 10740*

26 African American GIs taking part in a huge parade of American troops during the 'Salute the Soldier' campaign. The troops are seen marching past Nelson's Column in Trafalgar Square, London. *Courtesy of the Imperial War Museum. Ref. EA 18861*

In his autobiography, Eddie remembered the friendliness of some of the English people in wartime. For example, while on a walk through the streets of Scarborough:

> Everyone gave me a greeting, and some, more bold than others, even stopped for a chat. They wanted to know what part of the world I was from, and marvelled at the fact that I spoke English perfectly, and without any trace of a foreign accent. The high spot of my afternoon's walk for me was a darling old couple, who humbly begged to be allowed to shake my hand for luck. Until then I thought that sort of superstition was confined to uneducated colonials.[8]

Eddie died in 2007 at the age of 90.

Notes

1   Patrick Vernon, 'A true role model for this small island', *The Guardian*, 4 November 2009.
2   Patrick Vernon, 'Lest we forget those who died for our freedom', *The Voice*, 2–8 November 2009, p. 16.
3   E. Martin Noble, *Jamaica Airman: A Black Airman in Britain 1943 and After* (New Beacon Books, 1984), p. 18.
4   *A Charmed Life*, documentary, 2009.
5   Ibid.
6   Ibid.
7   Ibid.
8   Noble, *Jamaica Airman*, p. 41.

CHAPTER 13

ALLAN WILMOT: MAKING A DIFFERENCE

In 2008 Allan Wilmot happily participated in the launch and promotion of the Imperial War Museum's 'From War to Windrush' exhibition, where he told David Smith of *The Observer* (8 June 2008) about the hostility he had experienced in wartime from the southern white American GIs. The mix of racial bigotry and West Indian pride led to numerous fistfights: 'It was not done where they come from, the Deep South, where they had black and white segregation and talked about "niggers". When they saw us in uniforms they used to say "Goddam, look at those coloured limeys". If they saw us in a pub they tried to throw us out. You couldn't escape it.'

During the Second World War, Wilmot, a patriotic Jamaican and the son of Captain Charles Wilmot, a seagoing master mariner, served his king and country in both the Royal Navy and RAF. He was awarded four medals: 1939–1945 Star; Atlantic Star; Defence Medal; and War Medal. When Allan Wilmot enlisted in the Royal Navy, he lied about his age. It was June 1941 and he was just 16 years old: 'They wanted men – so when men are wanted, they turn a blind eye. We Jamaicans were pro-British. We felt British. When war broke out, it was a case of the mother country's in trouble and needs your help. And help was given, without a second thought.'[1]

After enlisting in Jamaica, Allan found himself on board the HMS *Hauken*, a minesweeper on convoy escort duty from the east coast of America to the Panama Canal. They also searched for and picked up survivors in the Caribbean Sea when cargo vessels were torpedoed by the Germans. Allan was one of only a dozen Jamaicans on board but, he said, 'on a small ship you become a family. You depend on each other – you're all brothers. There's no room for discrimination – in three minutes you could be at the bottom of the sea. Being the youngest one, I was more or less a mascot.'[2]

In January 1944 Allan successfully transferred to the Marine Section of the RAF for motor boat duty:

> In the RAF my unit picked aircrews shot down or ditched at sea. They could be any nationality. For example, we saw some airmen ditched in the Channel. Full-speed ahead, we went to pick them up. They turned out to be German

airmen, shot down. Anyway, being on the humanitarian side we decided to pick them up and continued to pick up the other British airmen. In the boat, they all sat looking at each other. I know what was going through their minds – 'Well, we are very happy to be still alive and picked up by a British rescue ship.'[3]

Allan felt that being black did make a difference in the Second World War:

I know for a fact that black American servicemen were confined to non-combatant units until late 1944 when the whole scene changed. All the black fighting units were suddenly sent over to fight in Italy and the Middle East to invade enemy-held territories. The black units were led by white American officers, until orders came from Washington that racial discrimination in the American armed forces should be discontinued. Then experienced black servicemen got the opportunity to move up the promotion to commanding positions. The British scene was different. There was no official racial discrimination in the services, but seniority promotion for a black serviceman was rare, even though you were qualified to do the job. They didn't want black personnel in charge of white servicemen.[4]

Eventually, Allan found himself in England:

When we landed at Liverpool, an air vice-marshal came to meet us. He said, 'Thank you very much chaps, for coming to help us.' That didn't last. After the war it was, 'Thank you very much. Goodbye.' The English were very, very curious about us. In Jamaica, we knew everything about the British Empire. But over here, they knew absolutely nothing. Once your face is black, you must come from Africa. We said, 'We are from Jamaica,' and they would say, 'What part of Africa is that?' At first we thought they were taking the mickey when they asked us, 'Where did you learn to speak English?' or 'Did you live in trees?' They didn't have a clue.[5]

However, Allan acknowledges that white civilians treated black servicemen and women very well. It was appreciated that they had left the safety of their homelands to face danger and help Britain in her hour of need. But Allan did not get along with white American GIs:

They were reluctant to accept the fact that the British black servicemen were a different race in social outlook. Many of the white American GIs were from the Southern states of America and, although they were in Europe, a very different social scene, they couldn't face the changes that took place. So we had open wars, especially in dance halls and various places of entertainment, with the local whites as back-up on our side. The black American GIs were a different story. We got along very well indeed. British black servicemen were their protectors.

At times they were attacked by groups of white GIs, especially if they were in the company of white girls. If they attempted to defend themselves against the white GIs, the American police were always at hand to arrest the black ones for the stockade, so we would go to their rescue and try to prevent them from being arrested. Because the American police had no jurisdiction over British servicemen, we could defend them – and ourselves – until the British police arrived on the scene, along with the ambulance for the wounded.[6]

After the war, Allan was turned down for the merchant navy, so he returned to Jamaica in November 1946:

But they weren't expecting us. No arrangements had been made by the government of Jamaica or the British military for our return. There were no victory parades, no preparations made. The British government thought it was up to the Jamaicans, the Jamaicans thought it was up to the British. Then they got some form of rehabilitation going, but I was frustrated and returned to England, where I thought the prospects were better because they were in the process of rebuilding the country.[7]

After a brief period as a customs officer, Allan returned to England with other ex-servicemen on an old troopship called the *Almanzora*. They arrived at Southampton on 21 December 1947. He worked as a postman, but was eventually drawn into show business. After forming a vocal group called The Southlanders, Allan enjoyed a long and successful career as an entertainer. His nephew, Gary Wilmot, also entered the profession and became a popular all-round entertainer.

In the 1980s, Allan became one of the supporters of the West Indian Ex-Servicemen and Women's Association. He was its vice-president for twelve years, and then the president. He also became increasingly frustrated with his visits to various war museums and libraries which failed to acknowledge the participation of black servicemen and women: 'We were left out of the history books, as if we didn't exist.'

Notes

1   Simon Rogers, 'Soldiers of the Empire', *The Guardian*, 6 November 2002.
2   Ibid.
3   Annie Keane, 'Making a Difference – Experiences of a Black British Serviceman', WW2 People's War, 2004, www.bbc.co.uk.
4   Ibid.
5   *The Guardian*.
6   WW2 People's War.
7   Ibid.

CHAPTER 14

BARON BAKER: A FOUNDING FATHER

Baron Baker was one of the most charismatic and outspoken members of Britain's post-war black community. When he died in 1996, Basil Jarvis of the Mangrove Trust, a black community group based in London's Notting Hill, remembered the impact Baker had had upon him in the 1950s: 'He was the first black man that I saw at Speaker's Corner in Hyde Park. He used to talk about issues relating to blacks in Britain.'[1]

Hubert 'Baron' Baker was born in Port Antonio, Jamaica, in 1925:

On Empire Day in Jamaica we were given a bottle of lemonade, we called it sugar water, and a bun, and we sang 'Rule Britannia, Britannia rules the waves, Britain never never shall be slaves'…When I left school I joined the air force to defeat Hitler. I was aware what Hitler stood for was to enslave me and my kind. We saw it from that angle.[2]

Baker joined the RAF as a policeman in 1944: 'There were people leaving Jamaica for America as farm workers but I didn't choose to go to America as a cotton picker or sugar cane cutter. There was a wider scope in the Royal Air Force.'[3] He was only 19 at the time, but he pretended he was 21 so he could be accepted: 'When I joined the RAF I found out that there were no black Commissioned Officers, and I took strong objection to this. Within a week of arriving we saw a black Commissioned Officer.'[4]

Baker remembered that, on his arrival in England, the vast majority of the British hadn't seen a black person before:

This is the first time they have ever set eyes on me and my kind. There were white people running away from us who thought we were monkeys, that we were something coming from a different planet. They didn't really believe we were human beings. The children played a great part in improving this because when we played with kids, they know you as an individual. Kids don't mess about with you as a collective group. Therefore when these kids come around the camp looking for Tom, Dick and Harry, they look for Dick, because they know he has a little sweetie for you. If Dick is on the camp, that little kiddie is gonna find him. When the parents see us get along with the kids, then they start to come nearer. As time goes by, things changed and the people's attitude changed and we lived quite amicably together.[5]

Baker recalled that the first major racial problem he experienced occurred with the American soldiers in 1944. In a pub in Gloucester, he and his friends were told by American GIs that 'back home niggers aren't allowed in our bars'. There hadn't been any problems in this pub before the Americans arrived:

> There was a vast difference between black English servicemen to the American black because in the Southern states of America if you're black you stay in the back. Some people call it racism. Some people call it apartheid. But to me that is naked, stinking, downright Hitler's fascism. That was something unacceptable to us Jamaicans. The American white servicemen who think they could take over Gloucester, we had news for them, because when they set upon us, we retaliate, and we retaliate in such a way that one night they had to use British laddies with sten guns to pick us up in town, put us on a lorry, and take us back to camp. When they parade us I told both our Group Captain and the American Commander that, 'listen, we are King George VI's soldiers, *not* Roosevelt's little black boys. We are not foreigners. We are British subjects and this is the mother country and you as a Yankee foreigner ain't beating us one inch from where we are.' We made it clear that if they put anywhere out of bounds to us we would fight them like hell. So both the American and English commanders got together and they realised something had to be done. There was some behind the scenes movements and it was agreed that our area was put out of bounds to American personnel.[6]

Racism was not monopolised by the Americans during the war. Baker later described the stand-off attitude of many of the WAAF personnel at dances they attended:

> At one of these bases where we were stationed we had social occasions which the locals would arrange. When we tried to get dances all the WAAFs would want to rest. But when an English airman approached them, they would take the floor with them. The situation was explained to the Commanding Officer and he issued instructions that WAAFs who didn't want to dance shouldn't attend dances.[7]

After the war, Baker felt passionately about the role West Indian servicemen had played in the conflict, as well as the sacrifices some of them had made for the mother country: 'Many of our blue blood blacks died for the establishment. I know it because I buried several in Oxford, so many of our young Jamaicans, and West Indians, contributed immensely to Britain's war effort. It should be remembered at all times. It should never be forgotten.'[8]

Baker was angered by the plans to send West Indian servicemen back home after the war:

> We were all right while we were in the air force, but when we were demobbed they wanted to forcibly send us back to Jamaica. All the West Indians should be forcibly sent home. They didn't want a black population in England. I said no way are they going to pick me up and throw me on board a ship. Let us give up ourselves up to the nearest police station and have this matter settled in an open court. The air force authorities didn't want that sort of confrontation and they climbed down from forcibly sending us home and they set up centres for us to train as mechanics, panel beaters, welders, and such like. I stayed on in Britain and was demobbed in 1948.[9]

When the SS *Empire Windrush* docked at Tilbury in London in 1948, Baker was there to meet it. At that time he was working as a liaison man with the Colonial Office and he had persuaded two Labour MPs, Fenner (later Lord) Brockway and Marcus Lipton, to open up Clapham South's deep air-raid shelter so that it could be used as a reception centre for the *Windrush* arrivals. The centre was only a short distance from the Labour Exchange in Coldharbour Lane, Brixton. Post-war reconstruction meant that there were plenty of job vacancies. Within three weeks, all the *Windrush* arrivals were employed and Brixton replaced the East End as London's main settlement area for West Indians.

Baker's impeccable war record did not help him in post-war Britain. He struggled to find regular employment and somewhere to live, but he finally settled in Notting Hill Gate in West London:

> We fought the war together. We win the war, then we must equally live together. That wasn't the way they saw it. The way they saw it, we come here, we did our job, a damned good job, let's kick them back where they come from. Well, we said no. This is the mother country and we come home to mother and we're going to stay here. We remained here.[10]

Notes

1 Maurice Mcleod, 'Farewell to a Founding Father', *The Voice*, 17 September 1996, p. 7. See also John Ezard, 'Columbus of Brixton reflects on 40 winters', *The Guardian*, 31 May 1988, p. 14.

2 *Black Britain (The Mother Country)*, BBC2, 7 January 1991.

3 *The Invisible Force*, BBC Radio 4, 16 May 1989.

4 'Baron Baker – The Man Who Discovered Brixton', *The Windrush Legacy: Memories of Britain's Post-War Caribbean Immigrants* (The Black Cultural Archives in association with Lambeth Council, 1998), pp. 16–19, first

published as *Forty Winters On: Memories of Britain's Post-War Caribbean Immigrants* (Lambeth Council/*The Voice*/*South London Press*, 1988).

5 *The Invisible Force.*

6 Ibid.

7 *The Windrush Legacy.*

8 *Black Britain.*

9 Ibid.

10 *The Invisible Force.*

CHAPTER 15

CASSIAN WAIGHT &
THE 'LEAGUE OF NATIONS'

In 1941 Cassian Waight, a 30-year-old civil servant from Belize City, British Honduras, volunteered for the RAF. With eight other Honduran volunteers he arrived in Liverpool on the ship *Orbita* on 12 September 1941. The others were Charles Egerton Eves (aged 18); Lewis Leslie (18), a painter; Raymond Lind (23), a salesman; Lee Longsworth (19), a civil servant; Orlando Pepitune (18), a civil servant; Lester Young (20), a shoemaker; and Pablo Zayden (23), a clerk.[1]

The ninth Honduran was Gilbert Walter 'Dick' Fairweather, a 19-year-old laboratory technician and the son of Major Donald Fairweather MBE. His cousin, Nadia Cattouse, left Belize City to join the ATS in 1943 (see Chapter 11). She says: 'Dick joined the air force and was a navigator. He was awarded the DFC. After a time spent teaching he asked to return to active service and became a pathfinder on a Lancaster but he was killed in action. Everyone at home heard about it. They were very sad.'[2] Dick was a member of 83 Squadron when his Lancaster came down in Holland following a raid on Wesseling in Germany during the night of 21/22 June 1944. The crew's flight lieutenant, Ronald Walker, survived and managed to contact the Dutch section of the escape route. He was hiding in a 'safe' house in Tilburg when it was raided by the Germans. He and two other RAF men, all in civilian clothes, were executed by the Gestapo. Dick Fairweather is buried in the Rheinberg War Cemetery in Germany.

By 1944, 'Cass' Waight had become a wireless operator/air gunner on a Lancaster with 101 Squadron. He was a member of John 'Jack' Laurens' crew. They were known as the K for King's 'League of Nations' crew because, in addition to the West Indian Cass, they had members from various parts of the British Empire, including South Africa and Canada. On 6 February 1944, Cass was promoted from sergeant to pilot officer (on probation).

In 1944 the crew were prominently featured in an edition of the BBC's overseas journal, *London Calling*. In addition to a photograph of the men (including Cass) on the cover of the 19–25 March edition, writer Carl Olsson told the story of their station in a three-page feature entitled 'Front-line RAF Bomber Station'. Olsson explained that the station only came into existence in July 1943 and that: 'The air-crews were over Germany the day after their arrival at the new station.' Wartime restrictions prevented the men in the photographs being identified, but Olsson did locate the station in East Anglia. He described it as:

One of Bomber Command's new 'front-line' stations, rushed up in wartime to serve the needs of our ever-mounting onslaught against Germany. From dozens of stations like it our bomber squadrons have gone out, night after night, to blast and burn the heart out of Berlin and the rest of Hitler's Reich.

Olsson also described the day-to-day life of the station and the conditions the men worked in:

Gone are the days of central heating and the comfortable brick-built living quarters of the so-called 'permanent' stations. With few exceptions these have been put to other purposes. And the RAF has been very generous in handing over the best accommodation to our American and other allies. Officers and men live alike in the same kind of Nissen huts dumped down on 'communal sites,' often with no such thing as 'water laid on,' and with a mile and more of unmade roads separating them from their messes and their working quarters. The nearest town with a couple of inns and one cinema is often several miles away; and RAF regulations, harder on petrol restrictions than most civilian authorities, allow no free transport to get there. Station entertainment is limited to a cinema projector. ENSA shows are unknown because there is no timber to build a stage. It is front-line existence as completely almost as if the bombers were operating from newly conquered territory. But if they grumble a bit (and who wouldn't) the RAF men grumble cheerfully and give their station nicknames usually based on the word mud. And they carry on, working harder than even the RAF has ever done before in its history ... WAAFs in the kitchen are cutting sandwiches for the crews, packing rations of chocolate, chewing gum, and milk tablets. In the locker rooms other ground staff are getting out equipment for each of the air-crew – silk and electrically heated clothing, flying suits, boots, Mae Wests, all the massive impedimenta each man carries with him ... The crews go from the 'briefing' to their 'operational meal' (usually an egg) and from there to the crew room to change into flying kit. They talk to nobody – except to those who were at the briefing – about their target, not even to their own ground-crews. An hour before take-off they are at their machines. And then at slightly over minute intervals ... they are signalled down the runway to join the great host from other stations at the appointed rendezvous, and then across the sea to fill the night sky above Germany with the appalling giant beat of their massed engines. 'Our bombers were over Germany last night ...'[3]

However, before the edition of *London Calling* was published, the 'League of Nations' crew had flown their last mission. In the early hours of 20 February, on a difficult raid on Leipzig in Germany, their Lancaster DV 267 crashed near Tolbert in the northern part of the Netherlands. According to Roy Laurens, Jack's nephew:

Jack, according to the five survivors, stayed at the controls of the Lancaster while it was in its death plunge to give the others time to get out. Three were too late, and died. Four of the five survivors fell into helpful Dutch hands and evaded capture for a considerable time. Royston was taken POW the day after they crashed. I think at least one got back to the UK un-captured.[4]

Tragically, Cass was among the three crew members who died because they had insufficient time to leave the burning Lancaster with their parachutes. 32-year-old Cassian Henry Waight, son of John Woods Waight and Lottie Evelyn Gladys Waight of Belize City, British Honduras, is buried in the Marum (Noordwijk) Protestant churchyard, which is about 12km west of Tolbert in the Netherlands.[5] Jack Laurens was made a pilot officer posthumously. Earlier in the war, Laurens had been awarded the DFM for his courage, skill and determination during a series of Berlin raids. He is buried in the Leek (Tolbert) Protestant Cemetery.

Notes

1   Source: UK Incoming Passenger Lists, 1878–1960, www.ancestry.co.uk, accessed 10 October 2011.

2   Nadia Cattouse, interview with Stephen Bourne, London, 27 September 2011.

3   Carl Olsson, 'Front-line RAF Bomber Station', *London Calling*, No. 232, 19–25 March 1944, pp. 14–16.

4   Roy Laurens, http://homepage.ntworld.com/billchurchley/laurens.html; and www.basher82.nl/index.htm, accessed 10 October 2011.

5   See Commonwealth War Graves Commission, www.cwgc.org; and The War Graves Photographic Project, www.twgpp.org.

PART III

AFRICA

CHAPTER 16

PETER THOMAS: THE FIRST OF THE FEW

In 1946 Robert Kakembo documented his wartime exploits in a memoir called *An African Soldier Speaks*. Kakembo, a Ugandan, had written this in his spare time while he served in the army during the war. In his memoir he praised another African who served in the war, Nigeria's Peter Thomas, and acknowledged what an inspiration Peter had been to other Africans:

> We have begun to think together as a race. We are all concerned when we hear of some unfortunate happening to Africans in some part of Africa or outside it. We are all happy and clap our hands when we see on the pictures in a cinema Pilot Officer Peter Thomas of Lagos, Nigeria, the first African to be granted His Majesty's Commission in the R.A.F. We are proud of him. He is one of us. He is an African.[1]

Nigeria's Babatunde O. Alakija was the first African to be selected for training as a pilot in the RAF. However, Peter was the first African to be granted a commission in the RAF and yet, in spite of this achievement, he is barely acknowledged in books about the Second World War, or the RAF, or black Britain. In 1994 Roger Lambo mentioned Peter in a chapter he contributed to *Africans in Britain*, edited by Professor David Killingray, but more should be done to acknowledge and celebrate this unsung hero from the Second World War.[2]

Peter, or 'Deniyi' as he was known to his friends, was born Emanuel Peter John Adeniyi Thomas in Lagos, Nigeria, in 1914. He was the youngest member of one of the wealthiest and most influential families on Africa's west coast. At the age of 17 Peter obtained his Cambridge School Certificate. He then attended King's College, one of the best secondary schools in Lagos, for another two years. After employment in his father's business, Peter entered the service of the Nigerian government in the Labour Department.

In 1940, after reading about the heroic achievements of the RAF in the Battle of Britain, Peter volunteered. He was supported by Charles Woolley, the chief secretary to the government in Nigeria, who personally forwarded Peter's application to London. In a letter that Woolley wrote to support the application, he commented that Peter was 'very anxious to enlist in the RAF' and described his father as 'one of the leading lights from the African community in Lagos'. He added that Peter's acceptance by the Air Ministry would therefore 'have excellent publicity value in Nigeria'. Peter had all the right qualifications for entry into the RAF; he was a long-distance runner and had enrolled in the Territorial Battalion of the Nigerian Regiment at the time of his application. Nevertheless, his application may not have been accepted if the casualties in the Battle of Britain had not escalated to almost 3,000 aircrew.

The British government had announced on 19 October 1939 that, for the duration of the war, they would lift the ban that excluded black recruits from the armed services. However, a colour bar remained in place in the RAF until November 1940 when the Air Ministry informed the Colonial Office that it would accept black aircrew candidates from the colonies. Peter set sail for Britain in February 1941, having obtained a passage on board the *Mary Kingsley*. He arrived in Liverpool on 2 May 1941 and was commissioned in mid-1942. *The Times* acknowledged that he was 'the first West African to be commissioned in the RAF and the first to qualify as a pilot'.[3] Dr Harold Moody praised this achievement in an editorial in the Newsletter of the League of Coloured Peoples:

> We congratulate Pilot Officer Peter Thomas, who came over to this country from Nigeria fifteen months ago to undergo his training for the Air Force and has recently been awarded a Commission. We understand that Mr. Thomas came third of all the candidates in a recent batch and although seven were required, there was some hesitation to award him his Commission, until he took further action about it. We gather that our young Pilot Officer is now waiting to be posted to our Operational Flying Unit. We wish him every safety and every success in the future. Peter Thomas, who is a member of the LCP, is the brother of Stella Thomas featured in this issue. It appears as if the Thomas's are out to set the pace in West Africa.[4]

In the same issue of the League's Newsletter, praise was also given to Peter's sister Stella, a founding member of the League in the 1930s, who did much to promote the organisation in its early days: 'Our heartfelt congratulations also go to Miss Stella Thomas, who has the honour to be created the first woman magistrate in West Africa ... Called to the Bar in 1933, she was the first woman Barrister in West Africa.'[5] On 11 February 1943, Peter was filmed by the Colonial Film Unit for a propaganda short to be shown in the colonies. No prints of the complete version of *Flight Officer Peter Thomas, RAF* have survived, but sequences were incorporated into *Africa's Fighting Men* (1943) which can now be viewed on the Colonial Film website, www.colonialfilm.org.uk.

Besides the RAF, Peter's interests extended to social welfare and labour problems, and he undertook other responsibilities on behalf of the Colonial Office. When West African social science students arrived in Britain for training, he took part in meeting the trains and welcoming them. He is remembered by Roy Sloan in *Wings of War over Gwynedd* as 'an interesting and somewhat unusual character':

He was the son of an extremely wealthy Nigerian dignitary, and was believed to be the only Nigerian flying with the RAF at the time. Thomas was an engaging and attractive personality, well liked and popular with his colleagues, and was exceptionally religious. Normally courteous and gentlemanly, he would let himself go at social events such as Mess parties after being persuaded to take a few drinks and would demonstrate wild African dances in a most impressive manner.[6]

Sloan noted, however, that Peter 'had a tendency to be involved in mishaps and accidents rather more frequently than one would have expected. It was rumoured that whenever he "bent" an aircraft his father would always foot the bill.'[7]

On 12 January 1945, on a routine exercise over the Brecon Beacons in South Wales, Peter was forced to make a crash-landing in the mountains. His companion, a young airman called Frank Stokes, later described what happened:

It was beautifully clear above the cloud ceiling and the exercise was proceeding normally and perhaps a little mundanely. After flying for some time, I noticed a sudden change in the light conditions. I looked up and saw that the aircraft was entering cloud: the pilot was descending. I think there was a fair degree of turbulence when suddenly the aircraft's engine tone changed dramatically, consistent with an attempt to gain altitude rapidly. From that moment events happened alarmingly quickly. I glanced up and could clearly see the mountain looming directly ahead of us, as pilot Thomas continued his urgent and ulti-mately futile attempts to climb. The port wing struck a rocky outcrop and the aircraft slewed to the left, coming to rest on a relatively flat patch of ground; I was rendered unconscious. On coming to, I discovered I was still in my seat, lying on my side. My shins were lacerated and my right eye and bridge of nose were cut. I had also received a compression fracture of two spinal vertebrae, but did not know about that until much later. I was not wearing my seat belt, as it was usual to undo the lap strap when airborne![8]

Frank then discovered that Peter had been thrown forward, clear of the aircraft:

He was lying on his back, unconscious, breathing heavily with blood oozing from his nose. He was a heavy man, but I managed with some difficulty to turn him onto his side so that his air passages were less likely to become blocked. I then had the idea to try and wrap him in my parachute canopy for warmth, but as I pulled the ripcord, the canopy filled quickly and the strong wind car-ried it away. I simply didn't have the strength to hold it. I thought about trying to set up a signal using the aircraft landing lights, but without any tools, this was an impossibility. It was getting very late in the afternoon, and I decided I could not afford to hang around any longer, or we would both perish from exposure to the elements if not our injuries. Thoughts of happier times passed through my mind as I looked at the desolation all around me. All I could see was the snow-covered mountaintop.[9]

In spite of his injuries, Frank made a painful and difficult descent and managed to stagger over 2 miles in the snow. Eventually he could see the road which led from the Brecon Beacons to Merthyr Tydfil. When he reached it, he discovered he was close to a youth hostel. Luckily there was a warden in residence, who was able to flag down a passing motorist who took Frank to the hospital in Merthyr Tydfil. Before he was treated for the effects of shock and had his leg and facial wounds stitched and dressed, Frank gave directions to the scene of the crash, hoping that Peter would be found. When two senior RAF officers visited Frank to conduct a preliminary investigation, he learned that Peter had not survived the crash. Frank remained in hospital for several weeks and was visited by Peter's sister:

…which was very kind of her considering the grief and anguish she must have been experiencing at the tragic loss of her brother. Perhaps she wanted to make sense of her brother's death or just meet someone who had been the last person to see him alive. She may have believed I had spoken with him after the crash, but that had not been possible as he was in a deep state of unconsciousness. She was an intelligent, perceptive woman, an undergraduate at Newcastle Upon Tyne University. I told her what I could about events and she went on her way. There was no further communication between us.[10]

At the time of his death, in anticipation of the war's end, Peter had already been admitted as a law student at the Middle Temple. Peter is buried in Bath (Haycombe) Cemetery and, in addition to his inclusion in the database of the Commonwealth War Graves Commission, his gravestone has been photographed and can be seen on the website of The War Graves Photographic Project: www.twgpp.org.

Notes

1 Robert Kakembo, *An African Soldier Speaks* (Edinburgh House Press, 1946), pp. 19–20.

2 Roger Lambo, 'Achtung! The Black Prince: West Africans in the Royal Air Force 1939–46', in Professor David Killingray (ed.), *Africans in Britain* (Frank Cass, 1994), pp. 145–63.

3 'Obituary. Fallen Officers – Royal Air Force', *The Times*, 30 January 1945, p. 6.

4 League of Coloured Peoples, Newsletter No. 37 (October 1942), p. 9.

5 Ibid., p. 14.

6 Roy Sloan, *Wings of War over Gwynedd: Aviation in Gwynedd During World War II* (Gwasg Carreg Gwalch, 1991), p. 63.

7 Ibid.

8 Frank E. Stokes, *The Story of an Aircraft Crash Survivor*, www.breconbeacons.org.

9 Ibid.

10 Ibid.

CHAPTER 17

JOHNNY SMYTHE: A VETERAN WITH ATTITUDE

In 1936, at the Olympic Games in Berlin, Adolf Hitler refused to shake hands with the African American athlete Jesse Owens who had won four gold medals. This act of racism angered many onlookers, including the young Sierra Leonean Johnny Smythe. He hated Hitler and everything he represented and when the war broke out in 1939, he decided to volunteer for the RAF.

Johnny was born John Henry Smythe in 1915 in Freetown, Sierra Leone, West Africa. He was born into a middle-class family who were known as Sierra Leone Creoles, descendants of settlers. At school in Sierra Leone his teacher gave him a copy of Adolf Hitler's book *Mein Kampf*, first published in the mid-1920s:

> I read what this man was going to do to the blacks if he gets into power. He vowed to use the heart of black people to make shoe soles. And he attacked the British and Americans for encouraging the blacks to become doctors and lawyers. It was a book which would put any black man's back up and it put mine up. I grew up with hate for this man and his cronies and was pleased when I had the opportunity to fight against him.[1]

Johnny's father wanted him to train as a doctor, but Johnny preferred to study law. In 1938, when his father was taken ill and was unable to pay his school fees, Johnny was forced to give up his law studies and take a job at the Freetown City Council where he undertook clerical and maintenance work. When war came in 1939, Johnny served with the Sierra Leone Defence Corps before volunteering to serve his king and country in the RAF. In 1940 he travelled from his home in Freetown to the Scottish town of Greenock, where he undertook training in the RAF. In 1941 Johnny went on his first mission:

> We knew what lay ahead of us. Every day we counted the number that returned. We also knew that there was a good chance that we would not return. We met with our first serious trouble during an operation over Mainz in Germany. The plane had several times been pelted by flak and it was in a bad state. Although we lost one of our engines, we still managed to limp back home.[2]

After nearly eighteen months of working as a navigator, Johnny, who had first become a sergeant, found himself promoted to flying officer. He was one of four out of ninety who was selected, and this made him immensely proud:

Standing in front of the notice board, I still refused to believe what I saw and read. An officer of the RAF! From that moment my life was completely changed. I no longer ate with the other ranks and I socialised only in the officers' mess. In effect, I was no longer one of the boys, although I often went to town with some of the airmen for a beer. Airmen had to salute me all the time. What made me so uncomfortable as an officer was not that I was the only black man to be promoted to that rank, but I was the only black man in the entire camp.[3]

Johnny acknowledged that the selection of his crew was extremely important because they had to work as a team: 'We were brothers in trouble, comrades in arms, and we needed to stick together and understand each other. We were posted to a squadron of the new Lancaster bombers; a plane superior to the Stirling.'[4] The crew's first mission was uneventful, but they dreaded their second:

Before setting out, I had my Bible in my jacket pocket and butterflies in my stomach. Every day we counted the number of planes that returned, and the thought of not returning to base haunted us. We went – and returned unscathed. During these first few weeks of operations, we averaged about three bombing missions per week.[5]

On one occasion Johnny and his crew were flying back over England when a German fighter began to dog them:

I saw it first and yelled to the rear gunner, 'Frank, open up!' It was quite scary because we were flying so low that, had the plane been actually shot down, we wouldn't have had time to bail out! The noise caused by the two aircraft brought our anti-aircraft fire from the ground, which fended off the German fighter, and we were able to land safely. Another lucky escape![6]

When Johnny and his RAF mates had time off, they relaxed together and had fun, but one day, in 1943, as he entered the mess with other officers from his crew, laughter broke out among the men:

Even the stewards joined in. We just walked quietly into the bar. Plastered around the bar were national newspapers with my picture on the front pages and the caption *Will they ban him too?* The articles reported an incident in which the famous West Indian cricketer, Learie Constantine, was involved. He had booked a room at a Central London hotel, but when he arrived to check in, he was refused accommodation because some Americans at the hotel objected to his presence. Constantine sued, the hotel apologised and paid damages. But the press and the British public were not amused.[7]

On his twenty-seventh mission, on the night of 18 November 1943, Johnny's luck ran out. He was the navigator aboard a Short Stirling III heavy bomber of 623 Squadron, one of 395 aircraft dispatched to attack the German city of Mannheim. The aircraft was crippled by anti-aircraft fire and the crew was forced to parachute from the stricken aircraft:

We were flying at 16,000 feet when the fighters came out of nowhere. They raked the fuselage and there were flames everywhere. Then the searchlights caught us. I was hit by shrapnel. Pieces came from underneath, piercing my abdomen, going through my side. Another came through my seat and into my groin. I heard the pilot ordering us to bail out. The pilot made it, but three of the seven-man crew were not so fortunate and we lost them. We jumped out and up to that point I never realised how seriously injured I was, because I did not feel any pain. We all parachuted and I landed among some trees. We had some rough ones before but this seemed to be the end. I have tried to forget that night.[8]

Johnny hid in a barn but German soldiers opened fire, spraying the barn with bullets. Johnny decided to give himself up:

I walked out of the barn and pandemonium broke out. The Germans couldn't believe their eyes. They were shocked to see a black man, but when they realised I was also an officer, they flatly refused to believe their eyes. What in the name of all Gods was a black man doing in the heart of Germany in what to them was a white man's war, they seemed to be asking each other. And they appeared to wonder whether what they had seen could be reconciled with Nazi propaganda; that the black man was sub-human and was at best the missing link between the Homo sapiens and his simian progenitors. I'm sure that's what saved me from being shot immediately. To see a black man – and an officer at that – was more than they could come to terms with. They just stood there gazing.[9]

After spending one week in hospital, receiving treatment for his injuries, Johnny was taken to Frankfurt for interrogation. This was his first encounter with the SS, or Swastika boys as he referred to them:

They saw me like a prized possession, almost a Gulliver in Lilliput. But the Germans were no Lilliputians, even if my own physical frame in some ways resembled Gulliver's. The spectacle of a black officer in the RAF was just not real.

Some probably believed that this was another example of the English sense of humour in its most grotesque form. I was only asked three questions, which were put with the proposition that as long as I answered satisfactorily, they did not care if I escaped. To all the questions I made just one reply: Smythe, John, No. 144608. Disappointed, some soldiers were ordered in, roughed me up and whisked me away to solitary confinement. The bed was a coarse and narrow plank, no blankets or pillows, and food was pushed from under the door. It was the end of November and winter had started to set in. My boots had been taken away. I had only a wet pair of socks which I could not dry or warm up for my frozen feet. I spent one week in this cell before my second interview, but remained adamant and was ready for a certain death.[10]

One of his interrogators told him, 'I want you to co-operate to get you out of this place', but Johnny refused to co-operate and simply repeated his name and number. His captor began to scream at him: 'You know they are talking about whether or not to execute you tomorrow, because you, as a black man, should not be involved in a white man's war.' When his interrogators realised that he was not going to offer them information, Johnny was happily reunited with his pilot and rear gunner and sent to a prisoner-of-war camp.

For the next eighteen months they were prisoners of the Nazis in Stalag Luft 1, a camp of 9,000 Allied airmen in Barth, Germany, a small town on the Baltic Sea. Stalag 1 had opened as a camp for British officers in 1942. American airmen began to arrive in early 1943. On his arrival at the camp, some trigger-happy German guards murdered several prisoners in front of Johnny for no reason: 'One day we found out that the Germans had taken away all the Jewish prisoners. There was talk of an incinerator being built just outside the camp in anticipation of a German victory. The effect on us was paralysing and demoralising.'[11]

At the camp Johnny continued to shock the Germans. Prison guards 'were dumb-struck when they saw me in an RAF officer's uniform. They did not treat me different from the other white prisoners. In fact, one of the guards was so puzzled by my presence that I was able to steal my prison identity card!'[12]

Johnny kept himself busy in the camp and enthusiastically joined the escape committee. He helped other prisoners to escape but couldn't break out himself: 'I don't think a six-foot-five black man would've got very far.' Then one day, in May 1945, 'we woke up and, to our utter amazement and disbelief, there was not a single German guard in sight. They had all abandoned their posts and fled.'[13] A few days later the camp was liberated by the advancing Soviet Army. A Soviet Army officer embraced him and gave him vodka:

> I was feted because I was black. They took me to a town near the camp and I watched as they looted. A pretty German woman was crying because they had taken all her valuables. I wanted to help her but the Russians wouldn't listen.

I had hated the Germans and wanted to kill them all, but something changed inside me when I saw her tears and the hopelessness on her face.[14]

After the war, Johnny worked at the Colonial Office in London. In 1948 he was at Tilbury with the black civil servant Ivor Cummings to greet the *Empire Windrush* passengers on their arrival. The almost 500 arrivals from the West Indies were mostly ex-servicemen. Johnny spent three years studying law with another RAF veteran, the Trinidadian Ulric Cross, while remaining an RAF navigator. He passed his law exams in 1950 and was called to the Bar in January 1951. After marrying his Grenadian fiancée Violet Wells Bain in 1951, he returned to Freetown. Johnny received the OBE in 1978, and in 1993 he settled again in England. Johnny died in December 1996 at the age of 81.

In May 1995, partly to commemorate the fiftieth anniversary of the end of the war, Johnny was interviewed at his home in Hale, Oxford, by Michael Butscher for *The Voice*, Britain's most popular weekly newspaper for the black community. The interview, entitled 'A Veteran with Attitude', was also published to help promote the publication of Johnny's wartime memoir, *An African Prisoner of War in Nazi Germany*, but it has proved impossible to locate a copy of this book. No copy exists in the collections of the Imperial War Museum or the British Library, and second-hand copies are non-existent. However, with his interview in *The Voice*, Michael Butscher is to be commended for helping to preserve in print the memories of Johnny Smythe.

Notes

1   Martin Plaut, 'The Africans who fought in WWII', BBC News, www.bbc. co.uk.
2   'African participants in the Second World War', Memorial Gates Trust, www.mgtrust.org.
3   Michael Butscher, 'A Veteran with Attitude', *The Voice*, 9 May 1995, pp. 15–16.
4   Ibid.
5   Ibid.
6   Ibid.
7   Ibid.
8   'African participants in the Second World War'.
9   'A Veteran with Attitude'.
10 Ibid.
11 Ibid.
12 Michael Butscher, 'Thank God, I Survived the War', *The Voice*, 9 May 1995, p. 3.
13 'A Veteran with Attitude'.
14 'African participants in the Second World War'.

CHAPTER 18

ISAAC FADOYEBO: THE BURMA BOY

In his book *Fighting for Britain: African Soldiers in the Second World War*, Professor David Killingray mentions Robert Kakembo as one of the few African soldiers to document his wartime exploits. Kakembo was a Ugandan who had become a regimental sergeant-major by 1944 and completed his manuscript in July that same year. It had been written in his spare time while he served in the army. The resultant memoir, *An African Soldier Speaks*, was published in 1946 and in it Kakembo describes some of the reasons why Ugandans volunteered for the army:

> It is clear that the majority of the African soldiers came into the Army not to fight for King George VI or to defend the Empire. No. The King and the Empire meant and still mean nothing to them. The men you see in the forces came to help a certain kindly lady missionary or a good District Commissioner whose wife plays with their children … There was another kind of African who joined the Army because he knew what German conquest of the world meant. This type of African had read or heard of what Hitler wrote in his famous book 'Mein Kampf', regarding Africans, and take it from me those men bore and still bear Hitler a grudge for having written the following words: 'From time to time our illustrated papers publish the news that in some quarters of the globe a Negro has become a lawyer, a teacher, a pastor, or even a grand opera singer … This is sin against reason itself; it is an act of criminal insanity …' The Africans who knew these words came not only to fight for the preservation of the Empire but to frustrate the accursed man's ideals and save themselves and their children from cruelty and permanent bondage.[1]

Many stories of forgotten war heroes have been highlighted in this book, but perhaps none of them are as moving as the story of Isaac Fadoyebo who, like Robert Kakembo, wrote a memoir about his wartime experiences. He was one of almost 100,000 African soldiers shipped to Asia by the British in 1943–44 to join the fight against the invading Japanese. This is now acknowledged as one of the war's most brutal campaigns. Isaac's extraordinary story of survival in the hostile Burmese jungle came to light when his memoir, *A Stroke of Unbelievable Luck*, was published in 1999 with the help of Professor David Killingray. He describes Isaac's story as 'a remarkable tale of human endurance but also a rare account of the heat of battle written by an African soldier. Although thousands of African soldiers fought on the front line in the campaigns of the Second World War, very few have described much of their personal experience in print or orally.'[2]

In 2011 the journalist and film-maker Barnaby Phillips successfully tracked down Isaac Fadoyebo in Lagos, Nigeria, and, after interviewing him, made a heartfelt and emotional documentary about Isaac's incredible wartime experiences. At the end of the film, *The Burma Boy*, Barnaby points out the one great irony in the story of Isaac and the other African soldiers:

> By recruiting all those African men to defend their Empire, the British in the end may have undermined it. At the end of the war most of those African soldiers came home and they brought with them new ideas, new perspectives. They'd travelled the world, after all. And those that were in the jungles of Burma saw that white and black were not so different after all ... we're all capable of courage, cowardice, intelligence, stupidity. We're all human. And as more and more Africans came to understand that, Britain's imperial authority was fatally undermined.

Isaac was born in 1925 in the village of Emure-Ile near the town of Owo, which is today in Ondo State in Nigeria. His home village was situated in rural Yoruba land and he was just a teenager when he saw the army as a 'good job'. In his memoir he explains that, without consulting his parents, and caring less about the consequences, 'I took the plunge into the unknown by getting myself enlisted in the army at Abeokuta'.[3] He now acknowledges that, at the age of 16, he didn't know what he was doing: 'They call it "youthful exuberance". That's why I joined the army. We were colonial people. There was no question of loyalty or patriotism. No, no, no. I saw people joining and I followed suit, not knowing that I was heading for trouble.'[4] Isaac enlisted as a volunteer in the Nigeria Regiment of the Royal West African Frontier Force (RWAFF).

Professor Killingray estimates that around 450,000 Africans from the British colonies served the British Empire throughout the war. Most of them came from the East and West African colonies. Killingray says:

> African colonial forces fought against the Italians in East Africa in 1940–41, in North Africa from 1940–43, and against the Japanese in Burma from 1943. A small number of African colonial troops also served in support roles in the Italian campaign of 1943–44.
>
> Many African soldiers were non-combatants, as was Isaac Fadoyebo, serving in the various specialist corps required by a modern army. African non-combatant auxiliary battalions, labourers in uniform mainly composed of non-literate men, built roads, unloaded ships, constructed defence lines, guarded prisoners

of war, served as head porters or carriers in the forests of Burma, and undertook the myriad manual tasks associated with the conduct of modern warfare.[5]

Africans joined the army for different reasons: a healthy diet, good clothes, status in their communities, and to try to earn money. The army also gave them a chance to see the world, giving them independence from their families and village life, which some found restricting. Such opportunities were rare.

From the start of the war Britain needed support from its colonies, but for many people in the colonies the British remained firmly in charge. During the war it was almost impossible for an African to become a senior officer and very few, white or black, questioned that. Regarding the white soldiers, Isaac says that not all of them were racist because there were exceptions: 'Quite a number were good … But some looked on us as black monkeys from the jungle.'[6] In his memoir, Isaac described a European warrant officer who tried to scare African troops by telling them they would find themselves in the jungle struggling to dodge the Japanese bullets. Isaac referred to him as the most irresponsible man he had ever come across during the military part of his life because his comments had a negative effect on the African soldiers: 'We had not the slightest regard for him'.

Isaac left Nigeria on a troopship in late 1943, sailing around the Cape because the Mediterranean was dangerous. They travelled all the way across the Indian Ocean before docking at Bombay:

> The journey took us six weeks plus. From Lagos to Bombay. It was our first experience of something that they call 'sea sick'. You wouldn't be able to take food, you'll be sneezing, you are not feeling well. But after a few weeks you get used to it. That was the only excitement. Very cool sea breezes. At times in some areas the sea can be very rough, very turbulent and at times very smooth.[7]

Isaac travelled with the other soldiers across India to the Burma border. At first he found it exciting, forming friendships, building camps. It was an adventure in an exotic new land, but the jungle was a tough environment: 'Very, very thick jungle. We don't have it here in black Africa. Very steep hills. You have to walk with a stick in your hands in marching order and with a kit bag on our heads. And if you make a mistake, if you slip, you are going to the foot of the hill.'[8] Killingray, who is also interviewed in the film *The Burma Boy*, says that West African soldiers 'were trained in carrying stores and supplies, ammunition, by head in forested areas … this would be very useful to deploy in the steep valley slopes in Burma. They performed rather well, particularly in forested terrain.'

In 1944 Isaac's story took a dramatic turn. His unit were getting closer to the Japanese, but they were unprepared for the horror that was to come. Isaac and his unit were deep in Burmese jungle having breakfast on the banks of a river, unaware that the Japanese were on the opposite bank and were about to open fire on them.

The attack on the river probably took place on 2 March 1944. Isaac vividly describes the attack in his memoir:

> Gunshots rang out from the opposite bank … we all ran for cover. A confused situation arose because we were badly positioned … we could not do much to evade the gunshots in view of the fact that we were on the slope of the river. The heavy fire continued intermittently for more than one hour … Each time the Japanese stopped firing, I made a number of abortive attempts to get away from the area. I did not know at the time that I had been wounded and I just kept on trying to move away. I was wondering as to what might have been responsible for my inability to lift myself off the ground and make a dash for shelter … My right leg developed aches and pains. So was the left side of my abdomen immediately below my ribs. I made an attempt to peep at my right leg and the left hand of my body and I saw a lot of blood. I then knew for sure that I had been hit by bullets in both parts of the body. I had a fractured femur very close to the knee and one bullet also pierced my stomach just below the ribs.[9]

Isaac was aware that in Japanese-occupied territory they did not take prisoners, unless you were white British: 'They didn't take us prisoner. They kill us. They came to me, two or three of them. The leader threatened me with a bayonet and said I should "get up, get up". They were talking their language. I can't get up. I can't even sit up.'[10] But the Japanese did not shoot Isaac and probably thought he was going to die anyway. After the attack Isaac was stranded behind enemy lines and close to death, but there was another injured African soldier nearby, David Kagbo from Sierra Leone. They comforted each other and were lucky to be near a village of Bengalis of Indian origin who, unlike many of the Burmese, supported the British.

It was these people who saved Isaac and David, risking their lives to bring them food and water: 'Maybe they were sent by God to come and save our lives … but it was Shuyiman who continued. He did so much for us. He took us to his house. Very courageous, because if the Japanese knew, they'd have killed him and killed us. They were very kind to me. They were sent by God to take care of me.'[11]

For nine months Isaac and David hid in Shuyiman's house. The Japanese never found them and in December 1944 the Japanese retreated. The British Army marched into Shuyiman's village and liberated Isaac and David. Amazed to still be alive, Isaac returned home to Nigeria. He had been to hell and back and was emotionally and physically scarred. He was given a 60 per cent disability allowance as a result of war wounds.

The reception in Lagos was overwhelming:

> As we were being ushered into waiting vehicles one could hear a band set blaring out 'For they are jolly good fellows'. Curious spectators … engaged

themselves in a stampede to catch a glimpse of us – world war veterans. From the questions people asked us they seemed to feel that those who were courageous enough to go into the battlefield for any reason whatsoever deserved respect and everywhere we went they gazed at us with amazement.[12]

On returning home to his village, Isaac received a second hero's welcome: 'If people have taken you as dead, and you suddenly appear, the tendency is for them to throw sand on you because by throwing sand on you, if you are a ghost, you disappear.'[13] The villagers threw sand on Isaac but he did not disappear, and his family and friends realised he was real, though nobody had thought he would come back from the war.

In *The Burma Boy*, an elderly Isaac is unable to make the journey back to Burma with Barnaby Phillips. There had been no contact with Shuyiman and his family since December 1944, but Barnaby decides to make the journey for Isaac, find the family, and personally take a letter from Isaac to read to them. Barnaby's meeting with the family of the now-deceased Shuyiman is an emotionally charged and poignant sequence.

After the war, Isaac became a clerk in the civil service and started to consider the possibility of writing an account of his wartime experiences. However, it was not until the 1980s that he finally wrote his memoir, typed out on A4-sized paper using an old typewriter. No publisher in Nigeria was forthcoming; but on the fiftieth anniversary of the outbreak of the Second World War, in 1989, the BBC's Africa Service planned to make a series of programmes about the experiences of African soldiers in the war. Isaac responded to an appeal for first-hand accounts and part of his memoir was incorporated into the programmes which were broadcast to Africa in September 1989.

With the help of the programme's producer, Martin Plaut, and Professor David Killingray, Isaac's memoirs were published ten years later and a copy of the original manuscript can be found in the Imperial War Museum in London. Isaac states: 'I don't like war at all. You will be killed. Some people will be maimed. Some people will be impoverished. Over what? As human beings we should be able to sit together and solve our problems peacefully.'[14]

Notes

1 Robert Kakembo, *An African Soldier Speaks* (Edinburgh House Press, 1946), pp. 8–9.

2 Professor David Killingray, *Fighting for Britain: African Soldiers in the Second World War* (James Currey, 2010), p. 143.

3 Isaac Fadoyebo, *A Stroke of Unbelievable Luck* (African Studies Program, University of Wisconsin-Madison, 1999), p. 17.

4 *The Burma Boy* (2011)

5   Professor David Killingray in Fadoyebo's *A Stroke of Unbelievable Luck*, p. vii.
6   *The Burma Boy.*
7   Ibid.
8   Ibid.
9   Fadoyebo, *A Stroke of Unbelievable Luck*, pp. 6–9.
10 *The Burma Boy.*
11 Ibid.
12 Fadoyebo, *A Stroke of Unbelievable Luck*, p. 58.
13 Ibid.
14 *The Burma Boy.*

PART IV

AFRICAN AMERICANS

CHAPTER 19

'THEY'LL BLEED AND SUFFER AND DIE'

This book is primarily concerned with highlighting the experiences of black British, Caribbean and West African servicemen and women in the Second World War. However, it is important to acknowledge the presence of African American troops in Britain. African American GIs in Britain from 1942 to 1945 are extensively covered by Graham Smith in *When Jim Crow Met John Bull: Black American Soldiers in World War II Britain* (I.B. Tauris, 1987). Other useful sources include: Juliet Gardiner's chapter 'Fighting a War on Two Fronts' in *'Over Here': The GIs in Wartime Britain* (Collins and Brown, 1992); David Reynolds' chapters 'Black and White' and 'Negroes' in *Rich Relations: The American Occupation of Britain, 1942–1945* (HarperCollins, 1995); and Neil A. Wynn's '"Race War": Black American GIs and West Indians in Britain during the Second World War', published in *Immigrants and Minorities* (Vol. 24, No. 3, November 2006, pp. 324–46).

The following is a summary of the experiences of African American GIs who began to arrive in Britain in May 1942 shortly after America had entered the war in December 1941.

During the Second World War around 3 million American service personnel came to Britain. Among them were 130,000 African Americans who were segregated and subjected to an appalling degree of discrimination that travelled with them across the Atlantic with their white compatriots. By 12 May 1942 there were only 811 African American GIs in Britain, but by the end of 1942 the figure had risen to 7,315. Until 1942, the majority of white Britons had not come into contact with black people, but during the war most of them encountered the African American GIs, or at least heard about them. The British public was also confronted with America's racial segregation policies and racist attitudes, especially those held by citizens of the southern states. Unlike their British comrades, American troops were segregated, and remained that way until 1948 when a presidential order from Harry S. Truman put an end to it.

When African American men began to enlist in the army in 1940 they were trained almost entirely for non-combatant roles, such as labourers, transport operators, stevedores, kitchen and domestic staff and stewards. They were not permitted to enlist in the Army Air Corps or in the Marine Corps. In Britain, the practice of racial segregation continued after the American armed forces arrived.

Black and white troops were to be kept separate, but 'equal', at work and while they were off duty.

On their arrival in Britain in 1942, white American troops were cautioned about making racist comments in the presence of the British public, and they had to be informed that racial segregation on the scale they had in the United States did not exist in Britain. A colour bar existed in some public places, such as public houses or hotels, but Britain did not racially segregate the public on transport or in restaurants as they did throughout the southern states of America, and in some of the northern states.

In 'Over Here': The GIs in Wartime Britain, Juliet Gardiner says that officially the British government distanced itself from the US Army's policy of racial segregation:

> But if there was no official support for the US measures of segregation, there were many in government and local administration who were anxious to place strict limits on contacts between the black US troops and the British population, particularly the female population. In August 1942, a conference at the War Office in London agreed that British officers should explain American racial attitudes so that their own troops, especially those women who were members of the ATS, might avoid contact with black GIs ... The British government was balancing on a knife edge – covertly supporting US Army segregation while overtly declining to assist in implementing it.[1]

Many British people were upset by the appalling treatment of African American GIs who, in their opinion, had come to Britain to help them fight against Hitler and Nazism. An unidentified Cambridge man expressed his disgust: 'I think the treatment of the coloured races of the US Army etc by the white fellows is disgusting. The coloured are prohibited from going to certain pubs, dancing halls, cinemas, just because the white fellows are snobbish. After all, both races are doing the same job of work.'[2]

An unidentified Birmingham man also expressed his shock at the racism he witnessed on the streets of his city: 'I have personally seen the American troops kick, and I mean, kick coloured soldiers off the pavements, and when asked why, reply "stinking black pigs" or "black trash" or "uppity niggers".'[3] The white GIs did not restrict their violence to their black countrymen, either. In 1943 a West Indian airman sat with his (white) comrades in a canteen for Allied troops when an American airman walked in:

> [And] seeing the coloured airman quietly sitting at a table, strolled up to him and slashed [slapped] him across the face! Of course everyone jumped up ready for a fight but the proprietress managed to stop it. Someone said 'send for the U.S. police' but the Americans tried to pass it off, and said that if the coloured man

would go, everything would be all right. The British said if anyone ought to go it was the American. A schoolmistress who was helping at the back, dashed out and slashed [slapped] the American's face, and her language was very choice! Anyway, they smuggled him out, but our men said if they saw him again they'd kill him … Meanwhile the coloured man sat there as if dazed, it was unexpected and so unwarranted. It seems amazing that the Americans are fighting on our side, when you hear things like that.[4]

It was not uncommon for black Britons and West Indians in Britain who were fighting fascism to find themselves the subject of racist taunts and violence from visiting white American GIs. In 1942, when the problem was brought to the attention of the government, the Colonial Office recommended that they wear a badge to differentiate them from African American GIs, and to give them some protection from the bigots. Harold Macmillan MP supported the idea and suggested 'a little Union Jack to wear in their buttonholes'. Needless to say, the idea came to nothing.[5]

At a Cabinet meeting in October 1942, Lord Salisbury spoke of the increasing difficulties and informed everyone about a black civil servant from the Colonial Office who had recently been refused a table at a restaurant he regularly frequented because American officers had complained about his presence. Philip Ziegler's *London at War 1939–1945* gives Winston Churchill's response: 'That's all right,' commented the prime minister, 'if he takes a banjo with him they'll think he's one of the band!'[6]

In many instances, when 'official' support or protection was absent, individuals took their own stand against the Americans. Jack Artis, a black British Army sergeant, born in Worcester in 1918, loathed the white American GIs: 'We were there to fight the Nazis, who believed in white supremacy, so God alone knows what they [the GIs] thought they were fighting for.'[7]

However, some white Britons might just as well have come from Alabama or Mississippi. On 6 September 1942 the *Sunday Pictorial* published an article with the headline 'Vicar's Wife Insults Our Allies'. In Worle, Weston-super-Mare, the vicar's wife, Mrs May, presented local women with a 'six-point code' which she advised them to follow if any African American GIs came to their village. These (in her own words) were the rules Mrs May laid down:

1. If a local woman keeps a shop and a coloured soldier enters, she must serve him, but she must do it as quickly as possible and indicate that she does not desire him to come there again.

2. If she is in a cinema and notices a coloured soldier next to her, she moves to another seat immediately.

3. If she is walking on the pavement and a coloured soldier is coming towards her, she crosses to the other pavement.

4. If she is in a shop and a coloured soldier enters, she leaves as soon as she has made her purchase or before that if she is in a queue.

5. White women, of course, must have no social relationship with coloured troops.

6. On no account must coloured troops be invited to the homes of white women.

To their credit, the women of the village were angered by this and refused to adopt the code which they found insulting. A local woman told the *Sunday Pictorial*: 'I was disgusted, and so were most of the women. We have no intention of agreeing to her decree.' The *Sunday Pictorial* made the following assurance to the black GIs:

> Any coloured soldier who reads this may rest assured that there is no colour bar in this country and that he is as welcome as any other Allied soldier. He will find that the vast majority of people have nothing but repugnance for the narrow-minded uninformed prejudices expressed by the vicar's wife. There is – and will be – no persecution of coloured people in Britain.

The persecution of black GIs from some of their white compatriots began to escalate as their numbers increased. By D-Day, 6 June 1944, it was estimated that there were around 130,000 black GIs based in Britain. In July 1944, after a number of minor clashes, a major confrontation between over 400 black soldiers and military police in Bristol city centre 'exploded' into a full-scale riot. Professor Neil A. Wynn says:

> Although the Bristol *Evening Post* dismissed the event as merely 'Local Fracas', and made no mention of its racial dimension, the streets had to be closed off with buses, and 120 military policemen were used to quell the unrest. One African American was killed and dozens were wounded. According to some reports a number of local people had encouraged the African Americans during the fighting: elsewhere they were said to have joined in against white Americans. As one reporter to the British American Liaison Board noted 'it was probably quite true that the British people sided with the Negroes simply because they always side with those they consider to be the underdogs'.[8]

One of the main causes of tension was the mixing of black GIs with white women. Professor Neil A. Wynn says: 'In the view of some British people, African Americans, like the rest of their countrymen, were not just "Over Paid, Over Fed", but also "Over Sexed and Over Here".'[9] In *Rich Relations: The American Occupation of Britain, 1942–1945*, David Reynolds notes that official reports showed the British public disapproved of racial mixing, and quotes the strong reaction of novelist Ann Meader: 'in the hothouse atmosphere of Weston-Super-Mare in October 1942, [she] was appalled to see two black GIs with two fair-haired white girls. She felt for a moment that the girls should be "shot" for risking "coloured blood" in their children.'[10]

Professor Wynn comments:

> Inevitably, some illegitimate children resulted from these wartime sexual encounters and they became known as 'Brown Babies'. Estimates of the number of such children born to black and white couples range from 500 to 2,000 ... The fate of most of these children is uncertain: some were placed in orphanages, others were brought up by their mothers or relatives.[11]

In 1945 the US Army finally permitted black members of the Women's Army Corps (WAC) to serve overseas. They were an all-black unit called the 6888th Central Postal Directory Battalion. Based in Birmingham, and later in France, their job was to route mail to millions of service personnel based in Europe; much of it had been piling up in English warehouses. The commander of the unit was Major Charity Adams, the first African American to be commissioned an officer in the WAC (in August 1942) and one of only two black women to hold a wartime rank in the WAC as high as a major. When the 6888th postal unit arrived in Birmingham, incorporating over 700 women, they were the first black women many white people in the city had ever seen. The women shattered the stereotypes, for the only African American women the British public had been exposed to until then were comical mammies and maids in Hollywood movies. They were given a rousing welcome when they arrived. Crowds of locals came out to watch as the parade of uniformed black women passed by.

To summarise, most African American servicemen and women were given a warm welcome in Britain. Professor Phillip McGuire says:

> It was generally considered – by British public opinion and by American travellers and journalists – that most British people accepted black soldiers as American soldiers without regard to race and color; however, the problem lay in the importation of American racial patterns to Britain by American white troops, resulting in clashes, ideological and physical, between American soldiers. Thus black troops felt that, instead of leaving problems of this sort at home, the [white] Americans tried to instill their ways and actions over here.[12]

Although the white Americans did try to instil their ways and actions on the British public, it is to their credit that the majority of Britons resisted. Juliet Gardiner, in *Wartime Britain 1939–1945*, recounts the memories of Mary Kemp, who was at a dance in her home town in Somerset when a group of black GIs arrived:

> Nobody talked to them. We thought it was very rude so we decided to ask the band to play a Palais Glide and make it a 'ladies' choice', and my sister and I and

some friends went over to ask them to dance, which they did. And that broke the ice. But afterwards someone came up to my father and asked him what his daughters were doing dancing with coloured troops. My father replied that he was proud of us. 'They're our allies too,' he said. 'They'll bleed and suffer and die, just like the white men.'[13]

Notes

1 Juliet Gardiner, *'Over Here': The GIs in Wartime Britain* (Collins and Brown, 1992), p. 150.

2 Ibid., p. 154.

3 Ibid.

4 David Reynolds, *Rich Relations: The American Occupation of Britain, 1942–1945* (HarperCollins, 1995), p. 303.

5 Harold Macmillan memorandum, 14 September 1942, Public Record Office, CO 876/14.

6 Philip Ziegler, *London at War 1939–1945* (Sinclair-Stevenson, 1995), p. 218.

7 Jack Artis, 'My Black Uncle', WW2 People's War, www.bbc.co.uk.

8 Neil A. Wynn, '"Race War": Black American GIs and West Indians in Britain during the Second World War', *Immigrants and Minorities*, Vol. 24, No. 3, November 2006, pp. 333–4.

9 Ibid., p. 337.

10 Reynolds, *Rich Relations*, p. 307.

11 Wynn, 'Race War', pp. 338–9.

12 Phillip McGuire, *Taps for a Jim Crow Army: Letters from Black Soldiers in World War II* (ABC-Clio, 1983), pp. 228–9.

13 Juliet Gardiner, *Wartime Britain 1939–1945* (Headline, 2004), p. 484.

POSTSCRIPT
IN MEMORIAM

Some black servicemen who were killed during the Second World War have been acknowledged in various chapters in this book. This section pays tribute to some others who made the ultimate sacrifice for their king and country.

For more information, see the Commonwealth War Graves Commission (www.cwgc.org) and www.caribbeanaircrew-ww2.com.

1941: Able Seaman James Bailey (Merchant Navy)

Able Seaman James Bailey of the SS *Western Chief* was born in 1915, the son of Marcus and Lilian Bailey. During the war his sister, Lilian Bader, served in the WAAF (see Chapter 3). He is remembered with honour at the Tower Hill Memorial in London.

1941: Galley Boy Tommy Douglas (Merchant Navy)

Merchant navy galley boy David Thomas 'Tommy' Douglas of the SS *Hawkinge* (London) was born in Cardiff in 1926, the son of Amizah and Sarah Ann Douglas. Lying about his age, he went to sea at the age of 14. He was just 15 years old when he was killed on his second trip on 27 July 1941. The *Hawkinge*, a British cargo ship, was torpedoed in the Battle of the Atlantic and sunk en route from Glasgow to Lisbon in Convoy Og-69. She was carrying a cargo of 2,806 tons of coal when she was torpedoed by German submarine U-203 and sunk. Fifteen men were lost out of a crew of thirty-one.

In 2002, more than fifty years after his death, the five surviving siblings of Tommy Douglas were presented with his three medals. The presentation of the medals took place in Butetown, Cardiff, and Tommy's sister Patti said she only knew about the medals after attending a memorial service for drowned sailors. Elder brother Billy told the *Western Mail* (31 July 2002) that Butetown had lost a lot of its sons during the Battle of the Atlantic when British merchant ships were attacked by German U-boats: 'All those boys went – and they went without a quibble – to do their duty.' Tommy is remembered with honour on Panel 56 at the Tower Hill Memorial in London.

1942: Sergeant Victor Tucker (RAF)

Sergeant Victor Emmanuel Tucker was a pilot officer in 129 Squadron and originated from Jamaica. Before the war he had studied law in England. On 4 May 1942 his Spitfire was shot down over the Channel off Octeville-sur-Mer, north of Le Havre. The Spitfires were escorting Bostons to Le Havre and aborted the escort shortly before the bombing run. By order they flew a left turn, to which the pilots had protested, as this enabled the Germans to attack from the sun. Victor was just 25 when he made the ultimate sacrifice. The incident was reported in the June 1942 issue of the League of Coloured Peoples' Newsletter:

> We regret to announce that Pilot Officer, formerly Flight-Sergeant Victor Tucker, a Jamaican, has been reported missing since Monday, 4th May, after daylight operations over occupied France. Pilot Officer Tucker was called to the English Bar in 1938 after which he returned to Jamaica with Mrs. Tucker and practised at the Jamaican Supreme Court as Junior Counsel to Mr. Manley, K.C., one of Jamaica's leading practitioners and politicians. Victor returned to England in September 1940 and was among the first West Indians who gained his wings. He was attached to the famous 129th Mysore Fighter Squadron.

1942: Greaser Simon Vickers Johnson (Merchant Navy)

Born in Falmouth, Jamaica, in 1904, Simon Vickers Johnson found work in Cardiff as a seaman in 1919. He was lost at sea on 12 September 1942 at the age of 38 when the SS *Ocean Vanguard*, the first Liberty Ship built in America, was sunk by U-boat 515, commanded by the infamous Werner Henke. He is remembered with honour on Panel 75 at the Tower Hill Memorial in London.

1942: Able Seaman Wilmuth Young (Merchant Navy)

Wilmuth Young was lost at sea on 12 September 1942 at the age of 41 when the SS *Ocean Vanguard* was sunk by U-boat 515.

1942: Private Johnson Bamsi (Army)

Private Johnson Bamsi of the 5th West African Auxiliary Group, West African Army Service Corps and RWAFF died on 21 September 1942. He is remembered with honour on Panel 8 at the Nigeria Memorial in Nigeria.

1943: Pilot Officer George Nunez (RAF)

Pilot Officer George Albert Nunez of the 9th Squadron originated from Trinidad. He was the son of Albert and Georgiana Nunez, and the husband of Olive Adella Nunez. His sister, Pearl, came to Britain after the war and married the Trinidadian folk singer Edric Connor. George was killed in action on 1 May 1943 at the age of 32. He is commemorated on Panel 132 at the Runnymede Memorial in Surrey.

1943: Sergeant Leslie Gilkes (RAF)

Sergeant Leslie Francis Gilkes of the 9th Squadron, Royal Air Force Volunteer Reserve, originated from Trinidad. He was the son of Joseph and Octavia Gilkes of Siparia, Trinidad. He was killed on 3 August 1943. Leslie and his crew were on their ninth mission and were returning home when they were shot down off the coast of Texel, Holland, at about half past three in the morning. Leslie, his fellow gunner 'Willie' Welsh and the crew's engineer were never found. He is remembered with honour on Panel 150 at the Runnymede Memorial in Surrey.

1943: Aircraftman 2nd Class Percy Gale (RAF)

Aircraftman 2nd Class Percy Gale of Cardiff died on 12 August 1943 at the age of 38. He is remembered with honour at the Bone War Cemetery in Annaba in Algeria.

1944: Sergeant Bankole Vivour (RAF)

Sergeant (Air Bomber) Bankole Beresford Vivour is remembered by Roger Lambo in *Africans in Britain* (1994) as a Nigerian bomber who 'joined 156 (Pathfinder) Squadron at the height of the winter offensive of 1943–44. On the night of 24–25 March along with 148 other men in the Squadron, he took part in Bomber Command's last determined effort to destroy Berlin. The raid was not a success and the attacking force suffered the loss of 72 bombers. Bankole Vivour survived, to take part in an attack on Essen two nights later. On 30 March 1944, 156 Squadron's Lancasters took off again from their Cambridgeshire base of Upwood. This time the target was Nuremberg deep in the south of Germany. Nuremberg was Bomber Command's most disastrous raid of the entire war. German night-fighters decimated the attacking force and one of the 545 men who died that night was Sergeant Bankole Vivour. Of his crew of seven men only the pilot survived. Nuremberg effectively marked the end of Air Chief Marshal Arthur Harris's "Main Offensive" against Germany.' Bankole Vivour was just 24 when he was killed in action on 31 March 1944. He is remembered with honour at the Reichswald Forest War Cemetery in Germany.

1944: Sergeant Vivian Florent (RAF)

Sergeant Vivian Bertram Florent was born in London in 1921. He was the son of the St Lucian actor Napoleon Florent who had begun his career with Sanger's circus in the Edwardian era. Florent's theatrical career continued into the 1930s when he appeared on the London stage as an extra and bit player in the films of Paul Robeson and Will Hay. In 1941 Vivian joined the RAF and two years later he was promoted to sergeant air gunner. He was listed as a flight engineer on a Halifax which took off from RAF Pocklington on 8/9 June 1944, detailed to carry out a gardening mine-laying mission. The aircraft crashed after flying into trees at Home Farm, Seaton Ross, east of the village of Sigglesthorne in Yorkshire.

It is possible that the pilot lost control while trying to avoid a collision with another aircraft. All the crew were killed and Vivian, aged just 23, was buried in the Pocklington burial ground in Yorkshire.

1944: Flying Officer (Navigator) Gilbert Fairweather (RAF)

Flying Officer (Navigator) Gilbert Walter Fairweather of 83 Squadron originated from British Honduras and joined the RAF in 1941. He was the son of Major Donald Fairweather MBE. He was killed in action on 22 June 1944 at the age of 22. His Lancaster was picked up by a German night fighter over their target area in Holland and shot down. He is buried with his fellow crew members in the Rheinberg War Cemetery in Germany. Gilbert was awarded the DFC.

1944: Sergeant Arthur Young (RAF)

Sergeant Arthur Wilmot Young of 106 Squadron was born in Cardiff in 1923 and joined the RAF in 1941. On 30 July 1944 he was on a raid over Normandy but the mission was aborted due to bad visibility. His Lancaster PB 304 returned home with bombs and fuel but it did not reach its base. Somewhere over Manchester it developed engine trouble and crashed into the River Irwell in Salford. The full bomb load exploded and Arthur was killed along with the rest of his seven-man crew. He was just 21. He is remembered with honour at the Runnymede Memorial in Surrey.

1944: Warrant Officer James Hyde (RAF)

Warrant Officer (Pilot) James Joseph Hyde, a fighter pilot serving with 132 Squadron, originated from Santa Cruz, San Juan, Trinidad. He was the son of Joseph and Millicent Hyde. He was killed in action on 25 September 1944 at the age of 27. He was killed instantly when his aircraft crashed at Elst, near Arnhem, Holland. He is buried in Jonkerbos War Cemetery in the Netherlands.

1944: Private Tomasi Kitinya (aka Thomas Liech) (King's African Rifles)

In 1942 a 19-year-old Australian, educated in England, called Lieutenant John Nunneley, was posted to the King's African Rifles (KAR) in Kenya. There he met Tomasi Kitinya, aged 16, son of Liech, a Luo tribesman from the shores of Lake Victoria. John engaged him as his personal servant and a strong friendship developed between them. In 1944 personal servants were told by the KAR to either enlist as askaris (soldiers) or return home. Determined to stay with John, Tomasi enlisted as an askari. In Burma's Kabaw Valley, John led his askaris in an attack on an enemy position but they were forced to withdraw under enemy fire. In his memoir, *Tales from the King's African Rifles* (1998), Nunneley describes what happened next:

I made my way to the main track in search of the Intelligence Section and spotted them taking cover on the other side. Tomasi saw me, joy and relief written all over his face. Leaping to his feet he started to cross the track towards me. He had taken just five paces when the Japanese machine-gunner covering the approach to the chaung fired a long, long burst.

Tomasi was shot dead by the Japanese machine-gunner: 'Tomasi was buried close to the side of the main track, the "Road to Mandalay" which threads its tortuous way along the floor of the Kabaw Valley. A wooden cross was erected over the grave with his name, rank, and number roughly painted on it.' Later, when Nunneley requested a photograph of Tomasi's grave from the Commonwealth War Graves Commission, they informed him that 'Private Thomas Liech has no known grave and is commemorated on Face 3 of the Rangoon War Memorial'. Nunneley says:

This came as a grievous shock for I knew that the temporary grave's map reference had been properly recorded and reported at the time of burial … What I did not want to believe was the cruel possibility that road building bulldozers and graders might have pushed aside everything in their way – even graves, unknowingly – in the urgency of the British advance, leaving no trace.

APPENDIX I

A SHORT HISTORY OF THE WEST INDIAN EX-SERVICES ASSOCIATION

During and after the Second World War, black servicemen and women were often based in different parts of Britain, and in different branches of the armed forces. This often led to isolation from others, especially after they settled in Britain after the war, and later retired. Sam King (see Chapter 10), who joined the RAF in Jamaica in 1944, acknowledges in his autobiography *Climbing Up the Rough Side of the Mountain* that, in Jamaica, veterans of the Second World War, with the help of the British forces and Jamaican government, instituted the Jamaican Ex-Servicemen's Association: 'It wasn't until the 1970s that the West Indians in Britain began thinking of a comparable Association. We were all members of the Royal British Legion but belonged to different branches and as such were not seen as a group marching at the Cenotaph in Westminster on Remembrance Sunday in November.'

The first planning meeting of seven men was held at an address in Atlantic Road, Brixton, in 1971 and included Allan Kelly, Hector Watson and Michael Arnaud. Consequently, the West Indian Ex-Servicemen's Association (WIESA; later renamed the West Indian Ex-Servicemen and Women's Association) provided an organisation in which ex-service personnel could meet each other, socialise and share experiences. Members have also helped to raise awareness of the historical role of West Indian servicemen and women. Established organisations like the Royal British Legion were not equipped to deal with essential issues facing West Indian ex-servicemen such as employment, housing and rehabilitation.

The members of the Association had their meetings at the homes of ex-servicemen and eventually, when their numbers increased, organised monthly meetings that were held at the YMCA building in Great Russell Street, off Tottenham Court Road. Their next move was to the West Indian Student Centre, and then to 1 Collingham Gardens (Earls Court). The Association's first constitution was drafted by two members using the then existing Royal British Legion Constitution documents as a template.

Recognising that they needed a permanent base and building, the officers approached the London Borough of Lambeth which generously offered seventeen derelict properties for them to view and choose from. Through the guidance of ex-serviceman Theo Campbell, a resident of Lambeth, committee members chose 161 Clapham Manor Street. A meeting was held with Charles LeMaitre, a

Trinidadian (solicitor), and the committee were inspired and cajoled to develop a viable association.

In 1982 the Association was established as a legally constituted charity and on 19 May 1984 their permanent base in Clapham was opened by His Excellency R.F.A. Roberts, the High Commissioner for the Bahamas. A plaque inside says 'This building is dedicated to all West Indian Ex-Servicemen'. There were also branches established in Birmingham, Derby, Manchester and Nottingham. A service of dedication for the National Standard of the Association was held at Westminster Cathedral in 1986 and in 1995 members of the Association were joined by the Governor General of Jamaica and the President of Trinidad and Tobago to commemorate the fiftieth anniversary of the end of the war.

In 2010 Vince McBean, chair of WIESA, was interviewed by Patrick Vernon for his documentary *Speaking Out and Standing Firm*. He said:

> The Association was started by a group of ex-World War Two veterans who came back to these shores and encountered a whole range of issues and challenges that they had to address. So this was the vehicle that they established. The organisation was established in people's homes, where they had their meetings, and collectively they would deal with the problems regarding one another and from home, income, jobs, training, and re-equipping for work.

West Indian ex-servicemen had something in common and, after a period of time in Britain, they realised that there was safety in numbers and that by coming together they could share experiences and speak out more forcefully about the problems they encountered in the 'mother country'.

Thanks to WIESA President Neil Flanigan MBE and WIESA Archivist Laurent Phillpot for their help with this overview of the organisation.

Note: In the year 2010 WIESA changed its name to West Indian Association of Service Personnel.

'FROM WAR TO WINDRUSH' (IMPERIAL WAR MUSEUM, LONDON)

The arrival of the *Empire Windrush* at Tilbury docks in Essex in June 1948 brought the first wave of post-war Caribbean settlers to Britain. Today, the arrival is viewed as a landmark in the recent history of Britain, for the *Windrush* symbolises the beginning of the transformation of Britain into a multicultural country. Over the next thirteen years, many other ships would bring Caribbean settlers to Britain, the majority of whom came between 1955 and 1961. Less well known is that the majority of the 492 passengers on the *Windrush*, mostly young Jamaican men, were veterans who had fought for the mother country in the Second World War.

To commemorate the sixtieth anniversary of the arrival of the *Windrush*, and in recognition of the war service of the 1948 arrivals, the Imperial War Museum in London mounted a new exhibition called 'From War to Windrush'. It opened on 13 June 2008 and displayed historical material and personal memorabilia, much of which was shown in public for the first time. The exhibition explored the involvement of West Indians and black Britons on the front line and home front during the First and Second World Wars. Among the exhibits were pages from the *Empire Windrush* passenger list; the telegram from King George V and Queen Mary expressing their sympathy for the death (in 1918) of Walter Tull (the former Tottenham Hotspur footballer who became the first black British Army officer in 1917); photographs and testimonies from Cy Grant (see Chapter 6) and Connie Mark (see Chapter 9); Sam Martinez's passport (he was one of 800 men who travelled from British Honduras to Scotland in 1941 to work as foresters); and the MBE belonging to Sam King (see Chapter 10).

'From War to Windrush' was developed in consultation with Arthur Torrington (co-founder and secretary of the Equiano Society and Windrush Foundation); Colin Douglas (historian and co-author with the late Ben Bousquet of *West Indian Women at War*); Stephen Bourne (historian and a founding member of the Black and Asian Studies Association); Revd Dr Rosemarie Mallett (priest in charge of a church in Brixton); and Dr Hakim Adi (reader in the History of Africa and the African Diaspora at Middlesex University and a founding member of the Black and Asian Studies Association).

Many veterans attended the press launch on 12 June 2008 and reminisced with journalists about their experiences. These included Lilian Bader (see Chapter 3),

Sam King and Nadia Cattouse (see Chapter 11). Others included the Guyanese RAF and *Windrush* veteran Donald Clarke, who told Michelle Adabra of *New Nation* (16 June 2008):

> When I first came here I was surprised by how devastated London was, the bomb raids had left a lot of damage; all of London was smashed up except for St Paul's Cathedral. I wasn't badly treated by English people. There was a war on so they accepted you. After the war was when people's attitudes changed, as the Government never told the people what was happening; they thought we were coming to take their jobs.

Interviewed by Simon Assaf for *Socialist Worker* (21 June 2008), Clarke said:

> I was surprised by the hostility we experienced as we arrived at Tilbury docks. And for someone who was in the RAF I was shocked, because as colonials we had volunteered to fight for England. Although I was often homesick, I have no regrets about making the journey. I tell young people today to stay committed to their dreams, don't give up your goals.

Arthur Torrington, who also attended the press launch, told David Smith of *The Observer* (8 June 2008):

> The majority of the first Windrush passengers were ex-service. They had skills from the war – engineers, mechanics, fitters – but they had to do jobs lower than they were trained for. For the first ten years there was a lot of resistance and discrimination, culminating in the Notting Hill riots in 1958. After that things began to change.

FILM, TELEVISION AND RADIO

FILM

British film and television dramas have barely acknowledged the existence of black servicemen and women in Britain during the Second World War. Of all the British fiction films set during the 1939–45 conflict, only a handful acknowledge their presence. During the war, Noel Coward's patriotic and acclaimed naval drama *In Which We Serve* (1942) failed to include any black actors, or extras. However, just after the war, at the start of the comedy *George in Civvy Street* (1946), when the star of the film, George Formby, is demobbed from the army, a black soldier is clearly visible among the troops. He is played by the drummer Freddie Crump, an expatriate American vaudeville performer who settled in Britain in the 1930s. But there is no trace of Britain's post-war black actors, such as Earl Cameron, Cy Grant or Errol John, in any of the classic 1950s war films like *The Wooden Horse* (1950), *The Cruel Sea* (1953), *The Colditz Story* (1954), *The Dam Busters* (1955), *Reach for the Sky* (1956) and *Dunkirk* (1958). An exception is *Appointment in London* (1953) in which Dirk Bogarde, as Wing Commander Tim Mason, leads a squadron of Lancaster bombers and has a brief encounter with a black RAF officer played by a distinguished-looking but unidentified actor.

In 1979 the director John Schlesinger, in his wartime drama *Yanks*, pointed briefly to the tensions between black and white American GIs. In 1982 the British mini-series *We'll Meet Again*, made by London Weekend Television, focused on the activities of a white American air force unit in wartime East Anglia. In reality, African Americans would have been an important part of this unit, but no black actors or extras were visible. In 1995 *The Affair*, an American made-for-television drama, presented a black GI in wartime England who has an affair with a white woman. A partially British cast included supporting roles for several black British actors, including Fraser James and Adrian Lester. In 2007, in the critically acclaimed film *Atonement*, the British/Nigerian actor Nonso Anozie appeared in a small supporting role as the soldier Frank Mace, who in 1940 accompanies Robbie Turner (James McAvoy) to the Dunkirk evacuation. Mace is not black in Ian McEwan's novel, on which the film is based. McEwan describes him as a big man, 'broad across the shoulders', who has served as a cook. So this is a rare example of 'colour blind' casting in a British film, especially one set in the past. Perhaps the makers of the film should have been commended. However, in the film version, Mace is a marginalised character and it is sad that some of his best scenes were deleted. They were later made available to view as 'extras' in the DVD release.

In his book *Censored* (1994), Tom Dewe Mathews made the following observation of the famous 1950s war film *The Dam Busters*:

> Probably the nearest thing to a cinematic representation of blacks [in wartime] was in *The Dam Busters* (1955), and this did not show the British film industry's racial attitudes in a favourable light. At the end of a bombing mission the squadron leader (Richard Todd) climbs out of his plane, crouches down, holds out his arms and then shouts, 'Nigger, Nigger,' as his black Labrador runs towards him.

The 'n' word is used fourteen times in the script of *The Dam Busters*.

The following is a list of some of the television and radio documentaries made in Britain that have focused on the participation of black servicemen and women in the Second World War.

TELEVISION

The Black Man in Britain 1550–1950 (BBC2, 1974): A five-part series exploring the history of black people in Britain. Part four, 'Soldiers of the Crown' (6 December 1974), focuses on the Second World War and includes interviews with Dudley Thompson, Sam King, Sam Morris and Ivor Cummings, among others. Credits include Tony Laryea (producer) and Mike Phillips (series adviser).

The Promised Land? (BBC2, 1982): In 'A Question of Colour' (22 July 1982), the first of a four-part series, West Indian ex-servicemen and women describe their reception in Britain immediately after the war. These include Gordon Small and his wife Marjorie.

Passage to Britain (Channel 4, 1984): 'The West Indians/Black Britons' (23 May 1984), part six in a twelve-part series, looks at the history of immigration to Britain and includes an interview with Garth Moody. He remembers his father, Dr Harold Moody, and the League of Coloured Peoples.

Hear-Say (BBC2, 7 August 1990): A discussion programme with black participants from the two world wars, including Ernest Marke (British Army, First World War), Ulric Cross and Billy Strachan (RAF), Connie Mark (ATS) and Lilian Bader (WAAF). It also includes archive film of Una Marson, Learie Constantine and Ulric Cross in *West Indies Calling* (1943).

Lest We Forget (Channel 4, 8 November 1990): A documentary about black participation in the Second World War, including interviews with Billy Strachan, W. Vincent Gage, George Powe, E.L. Armstrong, Stan Hodges and Tony Daley (all RAF), Nadia Cattouse and Connie Mark (both ATS), Charles Arundel 'Joe' Moody (British Army) and Amos Ford (British Honduras Forestry Unit).

Black Britain (BBC2, 1991): A six-part series looking at the history of black people in Britain. Part One, 'The Mother Country' (7 January 1991), focuses on experiences leading up to and during the Second World War. Interviewees include George Bridgeman from Barbados, who joined the army; Hubert 'Baron' Baker from Jamaica, who joined the RAF; and Connie Mark, who joined the ATS in Jamaica.

Black Poppies (BBC2, 18 October 1992): This was based on a stage production premiered at the National Theatre Studio by a group of black actors who had interviewed a number of black servicemen from the Second World War. Filmed on the Broadwater Farm estate, the actors recount their stories and experiences. It was shortlisted for the Commission for Racial Equality's 1992 Race in the Media award for Best Television Drama.

Birthrights (BBC2, 1993): A documentary series about black Britons from history. 'Reunion' (5 July 1993), produced and directed by Frances-Anne Solomon, focuses on the recruitment of West Indian women into the British Army in the Second World War. Interviewees include Esther Armagon, Norma Best and Connie Mark.

In Defence of the Chocolate Soldier (Channel 4, 1995): Shown in the Limited Edition series, this documentary about racism in the US Army looks at the real-life story of Leroy Henry, an African American GI who was sentenced to death for allegedly raping a white woman while stationed in Combe Down near Bath in 1944. It includes testimony from the trial, archive footage and extracts from *The Life and Death of a Buffalo Soldier*, a play based on the incident.

The Call of the Sea (BBC2, 1997): A six-part documentary series about life at sea in the first half of the twentieth century. It includes an interview with Sid Graham, a merchant seaman from London's East End, who served in the Second World War.

Windrush (BBC2, 1998): A four-part television documentary series broadcast to mark the fiftieth anniversary of the arrival of the *Empire Windrush*. In Part 1, 'Arrival' (30 May 1998), interviewees talk about their experiences of the Second World War, including Connie Mark (ATS) and several RAF recruits: William Nalty, Noel Brown, Euton Christian, Dudley Thompson and Ulric Cross.

Brown Babies (Channel 4, 1999): A documentary telling the story of the babies born to African American soldiers and white British women during the Second World War.

Small Island (BBC1, 6/13 December 2009): A two-part television drama based on Andrea Levy's novel. It is partially set in the Second World War.

RADIO

The Invisible Force (BBC Radio 4, 16 May 1989): The story of the West Indians who came to Britain to serve in the armed forces in the Second World War. Interviewees include Sam King, Billy Strachan, Baron Baker, Eric Burton, Ivor De Souza, Vidal Dezonie, Glen English, Neil Flanigan, Sid Gordon, Victor Lawrence, Sid Reynolds, Arthur Rosario and Andre Shevington.

The Forgotten Volunteers (BBC Radio 2, 11 November 2000): Presented by Trevor McDonald, it features the words and voices of black and Asian servicemen and women who fought for Britain and Allied troops in two world wars. Interviewees include Cy Grant, Norma Best, Lilian Bader, Ulric Cross, Rene Webb, Cecil Holness and the historian Ben Bousquet.

EXTRACTS FROM THE WARTIME NEWSLETTERS OF THE LEAGUE OF COLOURED PEOPLES

Dr Harold Moody came to Britain from Jamaica in the Edwardian era and by the 1930s he was a highly respected community leader. In 1931 he founded the League of Coloured Peoples and this became the most influential organisation campaigning for the rights of Africans and West Indians in Britain in the 1930s and 1940s. He remained the president of the League until his death in 1947. Under Dr Moody's editorship, the wartime Newsletters of the League offer snapshots into some of the issues faced by Britain's black community and colonials. They also provide important information about individuals from Britain and the colonies, including acts of bravery and sacrifice. The following are a selection of extracts from the wartime Newsletters of the League:

THE COLOUR BAR: REACTIONS

George Price and R. Spiers both tried to join the Forces and were refused. One of them writes:

> Some years ago a young lad attempted to join the Navy and was refused admission because of his colour, although his father had seen service during the Great War. As you already know, my own experiences during the last few months have been very similar. Now ... instead of a burning desire for an adventurous career, there now remains a warm sense of duty, not so much towards the country as to the comrades already in arms; and although it would be easy to satisfy my conscience on this point and be conscripted when the time comes, I am not altogether insensible to the fact that there will be many other young lads like myself, in future years, who from temperament and possibly necessity will wish to avail themselves of the training of some particular branch of the Forces. Because of this, I intend at present, to resist attempts at conscription until some guarantee is given that any and every branch of the Services will be thrown open to coloured lads when the war is ended.

The other young man, quite independently, arrives at a similar conclusion. These facts are recorded here so that all may know just how much damage is done by this cruel, un-Christian and un-English practice. It must be abolished at all costs.

[*Newsletter, No. 7 (April 1940), p. 13*]

Letter to Dr Harold Moody from Malcolm MacDonald, Secretary of State for the Colonies:

> The standard nationality rule for entry into the Royal Navy and Royal Marines is that the candidate must be the British-born son of British-born parents on both sides. I am sure that any man of colour who, fulfilling the above conditions, now presents himself for enlistment, will not be turned away on the ground of colour. I have seen a copy of the instructions issued to the Royal Air Force recruiting depots. They are very full, and I am quite satisfied that under them any man of colour presenting himself for enlistment will get a fair deal … The War Office have assured me that if Mr. Price [see above: THE COLOUR BAR: REACTIONS] joins the Army he will stand the same chance for promotion as any other soldier, and that if he has reason to feel that he is being discriminated against, he can exercise all the rights of a soldier to claim redress. I am very glad to have had the opportunity of looking into this case. The general question involved is one in which I have taken a close personal interest, and you may be rest assured that I shall continue to do all in my power to ensure that no member of our Colonial Empire shall be debarred from assisting in the war effort on account of his colour.

[*Newsletter, No. 8 (May 1940), p. 18*]

COLOUR BAR AND THE AIR FORCE

Letter to Dr Harold Moody from Charles Evans (Air Ministry, London WC2, 28 June 1940):

> Sir, With reference to your letter of 17th May, 1940, addressed to the Secretary of State for Air regarding a paragraph which appeared in *Reynolds News* of 21st April, 1940, on the subject of the colour bar to entry into the Royal Air Force, I am commanded by the Air Council to inform you that it has been decided that, for the period of the war, British subjects from the Colonies who are in this country, including those not wholly of European descent, are to be on the same footing as British subjects from the United Kingdom as regards eligibility for voluntary enlistment in the Armed Forces, including the Royal Air Force. British subjects of non-European descent who are in this country are considered on their merits for service with the Royal Air Force, and several have been accepted since the outbreak of war. I am to add that a careful examination of overseas man-power

resources has been recently made, and that machinery is being set up in certain overseas countries for the local selection and entry of suitable personnel.

[*Newsletter, No. 11 (August 1940), pp. 92–3*]

BRAVE LANCE-CORPORAL

The War Office announces that the King [George VI] has approved the following award for gallant and distinguished service: MILITARY MEDAL

Asamu, No. 11787 Lance-Corporal, The King's African Rifles

During a raid Lance-Corporal Asamu showed conspicuous coolness; while under enemy fire he continued to feed and supply his Bren-gun; he remained in action until all his men were able to reach safety under cover of his fire, and then carried his gun to a reconnaissance truck. His example was an inspiration to his section.

[*Newsletter, No. 13 (October 1940), p. 14*]

We must congratulate Mr Babatunde O. Alakija on being the first African to be selected for training as a pilot in H.M. Air Force. We feel certain he will do well. We hear very good news of all our men now in the forces.

[*Newsletter, No. 15 (December 1940), p. 49*]

Author's note: Babatunde O. Alakija was the son of the Hon. A. Alakija, a member of the Legislative Council of Nigeria. Babatunde was educated at Oxford and held the British Public Schools High Jump Championship.

THE KING INSPECTS COLOURED SEAMEN

The *Daily Mirror*, of December 19th, published a photograph of some coloured seamen, whom they said brought 'food and munitions to us in spite of U-boats, mines and bombing planes,' and who were inspected by H.M. the King on the previous day. Among these we recognised Maxted from Barbados, and Prince from Jamaica. These seamen play a very important part in warfare. We hope they will not again be forgotten as they were after the last war, when the League of Coloured Peoples had to take action in order to get their nationality, which had been wrongfully abridged, restored to them.

[*Newsletter, No. 16 (January 1941), p. 99*]

Our Treasurer, Dr Christine Moody, on December 9th, joined the R.A.M.C. as Lieutenant. Her father, Dr Harold Moody, President of the League, on December 12th had the honour of being presented to the Queen at Buckingham Palace by the Rt. Hon. Lord Lloyd, Secretary of State for the Colonies, when he presented to the nation a number of ambulances subscribed for by the Colonies.

[*Newsletter, No. 16 (January 1941), p. 104*]

AFRICAN ENDURANCE AND COURAGE
(*The Times*, 10 October)

An example of courage, endurance and bushcraft is provided by the remarkable story of a young Gold Coast soldier who escaped from the Italians and travelled alone without food or water for five days and nights until he regained his unit. He was made prisoner during a raid carried out on a strong Italian position in thick bush. After the battle the enemy stripped him of everything except his singlet and shorts, and placed him under guard. Awaiting his opportunity, he broke away, and after running blindly for a long time through the bush, he awaited nightfall, and then set off. Five days later, exhausted, starved and suffering from severe thirst, he stumbled into a British outpost, having traversed many miles of hostile country, which was unknown to him.

[*Newsletter, No. 17 (February 1941), p. 120*]

HEROISM OF AFRICAN SEAMAN
SAVES A BRITISH MERCHANT SHIP

The story was recently told by the *Daily Express* of the way in which George Taylor, of Freetown, Sierra Leone, saved his ship when it was attacked by a raider. Though wounded in one eye and half-blinded in the other, he stuck to the wheel on the bridge and carried out his Captain's orders, when the ship was ablaze, and all had taken to the one lifeboat, with the exception of the Captain, two engineers, two radio men and the cabin boy. Taylor continued at the wheel and brought his ship safely to port.

[*Newsletter, No. 18 (March 1941), pp. 132–3*]

AFRICAN SOLDIER RECEIVES THE
MILITARY MEDAL FOR GALLANTRY
(*West African Pilot*, 18 February)

The Italians were shelling a British position in East Africa when one shell scored a direct hit on the post where Askari Willie was stationed. His C.O. [commanding officer] and two African soldiers were killed, four more wounded and the rest suffering from shock. Willie picked himself up and ran to a light automatic gun. This was out of action, but he soon fixed it and went into action. Without waiting for orders, he took command of the post, and urged the men who could stand on their feet to open fire on the advancing Italian Blackshirts. They were driven off and the post held until relief came. 'Askari Willie is every inch a soldier,' said the C.O. when presenting him with the Military Medal for gallantry.

[*Newsletter, No. 20 (May 1941), p. 42*]

BBC GREETINGS PROGRAMMES: CORRESPONDENCE
8th April: from Dr Moody to the Director, BBC

My attention has been drawn to the fact that in your *Good Night to the Forces*, while mentioning most of those who are taking part in the Allied cause, you omitted to include the West Indians of whom there are more than a thousand serving at present, the West Africans who played a very effective part in the Abyssinian campaign and the King's African Rifles who have also served equally well. I am quite certain this is only an omission in your part and if it could be corrected it would help to satisfy a large number of His Majesty's loyal subjects.

14th April: from the Director, BBC, to Dr Moody

The programme to which you refer is intended solely for Imperial and Allied Forces who are serving with us as part of the Armed Forces in Great Britain. This will explain why it is that West Africans are not included.

21st April: from Dr Moody to the Director, BBC

While you have explained about the West Africans you have not referred to the West Indians in Britain of whom there are a very large number. May I know why these are left out from your programme and if there is any possibility of their inclusion therein?

5th May: from the Director, BBC, to Dr Moody

If you listened to the more recent *Greetings* programmes you will have heard that the West Indians serving in Great Britain are now included.

[*Newsletter, No. 33 (June 1942), p. 66*]

Bristol Evening World, July 23rd, 1942

Sir: At a Monday evening whist drive held at a West Country church, some coloured troops were refused entry, although other troops were allowed. This incident was, in spirit, as hateful as anything out of Nazi Germany. I know that the majority of British subjects share my views on this question of colour-bar, and I trust they will show the erring minority just where they get off. JAMES CONSTANT

[*Newsletter, No. 36 (September 1942), p. 164*]

NO COLOUR BAR IN LYONS RESTAURANT

One of our members (English) and her friend recently visited the Strand Palace Hotel for a cup of tea. When they took their seats they noticed three coloured soldiers sitting at their next table. Subsequently a Colonel of the British Army and a Subaltern came in and occupied a table nearby. After a little time the waitress came to them for their order, as she was leaving the soldiers beckoned her. The Colonel retorted: 'You fellows must wait.' The girl immediately went to the soldiers' table and apologised to them for not taking their order first and proceeded to take it, whereupon the two officers left the restaurant. Such stories are good to hear.

[*Newsletter, No. 37 (October 1942), p. 14*]

TENTH COLONIAL CENTRE OPENED
BY THE DUCHESS OF GLOUCESTER

Colonial Centre, a hostel and club for Colonials in London, at 17 Russell Square WC1, was opened on Tuesday 9th March, 1943, by H.R.H. the Duchess of Gloucester … A guard of Colonials in the RAF included Pilot Officer Peter Thomas, first West African to be commissioned in the RAF. Others in uniform included Capt. C.O. Moody, R.A.M.C., and Captain Arundel Moody, R.A. The Centre is run and financed by the Colonial Office, and provides hostel accommodation for 35 residents. It is open to all Colonials irrespective of colour, race or religion.

[*Newsletter, No. 43 (April 1943), p. 7*]

Into a packed 'bus in Bristol, in which there were two coloured American soldiers seated, came two white American soldiers. They motioned to the coloured men, who rose from their seats which were then taken by the white soldiers. The conductress on returning from the top of the 'bus, and noticing what had happened, remarked: 'This is England and such things are not done here. These two men were on before you and seated, they must have back their seats.' She rang the bell and the white Americans chose to get off.
Bravo to our Conductress!! – ED.

[*Newsletter, No. 50 (November 1943), p. 32*]

COLOUR BAR CHARGE AT PUBLIC DANCES

An unofficial colour bar has been imposed at public dances held at Watford (Herts) Town Hall. Incidents have occurred in which Army officers have walked out when coloured men, many of them serving soldiers, came in. Girls have refused to dance with them. Alderman E.C. Last, chairman of the Town Hall Management Committee, said last night: 'If I hear of definite cases where dance promoters are operating a colour bar, I shall ask my committee to refuse further permission to hire the hall.'

[*Newsletter, No. 54 (March 1944), p. 96*]

WHY SGT SWEET GAVE £500 TO BEAT COLOUR BAR
(*Daily Worker*, 3 May 1944)

'I just don't like to see other people being pushed around.' This was the reply I got from Jay Sweet, lanky, blue-eyed, 28-year-old U.S. Sergeant film actor who has just finished starring in *A Canterbury Tale*, when I asked him what prompted him to give his film pay – £500 – to the National Association for the Advancement of Coloured People. Jay's present job is as clerk at the Headquarters of European Theatre of Operations. He told me that many of the fellows he works with feel the same way about colour discrimination as he does. 'I was surprised at the number of fellows who came up to me and said: "That's the swellest thing you could have done with the money, Jay."'

[*Newsletter, No. 57 (June 1944), p. 32*]

Author's note: John Sweet (1916–2011), from Minneapolis, Minnesota, was a US Army sergeant serving in the UK in the Second World War. He wasn't a professional actor but was spotted by the director Michael Powell and cast as Sergeant Bob Johnson, an American serviceman discovering the joys of the English countryside. It was his only film appearance. After the war he returned to America and resumed his teaching career. John donated his £500 salary to the NAACP because, as a serving soldier, the US Army would not allow him to earn money from another source.

SECRETARY'S NOTES

The British Empire Medal has been awarded to Leading Fireman G.A. Roberts, formerly of Trinidad, who is one of our foundation members and has been a member of our Executive Committee almost from the inception of the League. Mr Roberts served in the last war with an English Regiment, was an N.C.O., and returned to this country at the close of hostilities where he has settled down. Two sons, Cyril and Victor, have also seen service in this war. Cyril was captured in France before Dunkirk and has been a prisoner of war ever since. Victor is serving with the Royal Artillery. The award to Mr Roberts was made for general duties and for his part as a founder and pioneer of the Discussion and Education groups of the Fire Service. We heartily congratulate him.

[*Newsletter, No. 58 (June 1944), p. 67*]

Author's note: In the January 1945 Newsletter it was reported that Cyril, who had been a prisoner of war in Germany's Stalag 383, was playing rugby and cricket for England and attending classes in electrical engineering. Victor, a mechanic engineer, had just returned from D-Day.

Dr and Mrs Moody's eldest and youngest sons have just been called up. Five of their six children are now in the Forces. Garth, the youngest, has been helping in the work of the LCP during the past three months. Captain Christine Moody writes cheerfully from India: 'It may interest you to know the official list of offices which I hold – Staff Surgeon, O.C. Dett. 31 Coy. R.A.M.C., Security Officer, Anti-Malaria Officer, Officer i/c photography. They are my permanent offices. At the present I am also O.C. British Military Hospital, Quartermaster, Officer i/c Families Hospital.' No wonder she says: 'I have been very busy.' We trust these many appointments will not weigh her down overmuch.

[*Newsletter, No. 59 (August 1944), p. 72*]

NIGERIAN BOMBARDIER DEFIES DEATH TO REPAIR TELEPHONE LINE IN FACE OF ENEMY ACTION
(*West African Pilot*, 30 May)

NEW DELHI, May 29 – The drone of our aircraft, arriving to attack the position, could already be heard. The dive-bombers had been promised a smoke bomb to guide them. But the telephone line to the guns which were to fire the smoke bomb had been cut. A Japanese medium machine-gun had pinned everyone to the ground. To attempt to repair the line meant to risk death. Signal Bombardier Audu Bagarimi (NA. 29618) of Bagarimi, Nigeria, tackled the job. While bullets whizzed at him continuously, he crept along following the telephone line, until he found the break. He repaired it, orders were passed to the guns, and the signal smoke bomb was fired just as the dive-bombers arrived overhead. Their attack was deadly accurate and shortly afterwards another objective in the Kaladan Valley had fallen to the West African Expeditionary Force. Audu Bagarimi helped to win that battle.

[*Newsletter, No. 60 (September 1944), p. 91*]

WEST INDIAN PILOT OFFICER GETS REDRESS FROM USA ARMY ON THE COLOUR BAR

A West Indian pilot officer was struck in the face by an American soldier at an ATC dance. This officer did not retaliate, but reported the incident to the American Headquarters. The soldier was tried by a general court-martial and we publish here a letter from the CO, a Major-General of the US Army, to the pilot officer. (We made representations also to the Colonial Office and Air Ministry):

Private James H. Palmer, a member of this command, was tried by general court-martial on 11th July, 1944, upon a charge of assaulting you. Private Palmer was found guilty except that he was not aware of your commissioned status at the time. He was sentenced to dishonourable discharge, forfeiture of all his pay and allowances, and to confinement to hard labour for two years. As reviewing authority in the case, I approved the sentence, but suspended the execution of the dishonourable discharge until the soldier's release from confinement. It is a matter of regret that this incident occurred and that a member of this command was guilty of such misconduct.

[*Newsletter, No. 60 (September 1944), p. 97*]

THREE MORE WEST AFRICANS IN BURMA RECEIVE THE M.M.

The Military Medal has been awarded to Corporal Adama Gafasa of the Nigeria Regiment, to Sgt. Ali Yola of the Reconnaissance Regiment (Nigeria), and to Trooper Robert Lamaire of the Reconnaissance Regiment (Sierra Leone). These three men each showed outstanding courage in the face of the enemy, the Corporal and the Sergeant each leading and rallying his section against fierce opposition, and with disregard for his own personal safety. Trooper Lamaire was engaged with his section in an out-flanking attack on an enemy position. Despite intensive fire from all directions he ran into the open five times, throwing grenades at a distance of five yards from the enemy. During the withdrawal he went forward under fire and recovered the body of a wounded African Corporal. On his way back he was ambushed but continued to carry his wounded comrade to where help could be given.

[*Newsletter, No. 61 (October 1944), p. 11*]

SECRETARY'S NOTES

The 2,000 West Indian members of the R.A.F. who arrived recently in this country are now undergoing training in different parts of the country. From letters I have received they appear to be very happy ... The Duke of Devonshire has been entertaining groups of West Indian A.T.S. girls, who have recently arrived, to tea at the Colonial Office. I am not sure of the number of girls who have arrived for this service, but I understand that the number is 'comparatively large' and more are on their way. The girls seem to be doing well too. In a letter I read from one Jamaican member, she says:

I am happy to say we are all well and enjoying every minute of the camp life. We have made lots of friends here since we came; the girls are simply sweet to us. We told them all about Jamaica and its people. One girl was shocked to learn that there isn't any snow in Jamaica. I am sure I'll enjoy my stay here; it's too bad it won't be for long; just the same I hope I'll be posted to a place where I shall be as happy.

[*Newsletter, No. 61 (October 1944), p. 19*]

WEST AFRICANS HEROES IN BATTLE FOR ITALY
(*Nigerian Observer*, 4 August)

It has just been announced that West African troops are sharing in the battle of Italy. The first account of their thrilling experiences has now been received, and shows that on this front, as in Burma, they have been doing excellent work under the grimmest battle conditions. It is revealed that detachments of West African nursing orderlies took part in the landings on the beaches of Augusta on the east coast of Sicily, and Salerno, in Italy, and with great coolness and efficiency tended the evacuated casualties under very heavy shellfire and bombing from the air. Pioneers were also among the West African troops.

Since the landings the West Africans have advanced with the victorious Allied forces, and have been bombed from the air several times at such places as Naples and Bari. The secret of their role in the Italian campaign has been well kept, for in their ten months they have nursed English, Scots, Indians, South Africans, French, Poles and Yugoslavs, besides other Africans such as Basuto, Bechuana and Swazi and a number of Germans.

There are four West African Medical Units operating in Italy, two sections and two self-contained units designed to deal exclusively with African patients. All personnel are trained nursing orderlies of the West African Army Medical Corps and Pioneers of the Royal West Africa Frontier Force, most of whom are from Southern Nigeria and the Cameroons, who perform general duties. Each unit is attached to a British General Hospital, and is under the charge of a British Medical Officer.

Their officers speak highly of their knowledge and ability. The men are housed and fed exactly like their British comrades, and as special officer have Captain Tomlinson, who went from Nigeria with the West Africans, and visits the detachments regularly to supervise their welfare and help with their family affairs. A rest camp for their use has been opened outside Naples.

[Newsletter, No. 62 (November 1944), p. 41]

SECRETARY'S NOTES

Thousands of West Indians have been arriving in this country for the RAF. They were recruited at home for the ground trade of flight mechanic. They all left their homes with the usual flag waving parades to the tune of the local militia bands and Governor's speeches – a memorable occasion. A month after the arrival of the first contingent, the Secretary of State for the Colonies visited their camp and they were again told how they would contribute to the overthrow of this evil thing, Fascism.

For most of them, coming over here meant adventure; of course, they knew it meant sacrifice, too. However, their spirits were high and they were prepared for anything from the enemy.

Less than six months after their arrival, however, they have become disillusioned and dissatisfied. Their first disappointment was the announcement that recruiting for the trade of flight mechanic for which they came had ceased since January, on the orders of the Air Ministry. Yet these men were quite ready to adapt themselves to some useful job; this was not to be – most of them were put on general duties and given the most menial jobs. A few were made clerks, and others were given the routine duties – one group had to take all the black-out down and put it up again.

The climax came, however, when a few WAAF 'collaborationists' told some of the lads that they had received instructions not to be seen with them 'because of the Americans.' Four of these girls are alleged to have been posted because they refused to obey the order.

In all the conversations I have had with these airmen they always assured me they did not believe these orders were given by the Air Ministry. The local officers and NCOs seemed to be responsible for most of the trouble. It is about time the authorities in this country debunked this 'American bogey' which is now being used as an excuse for every discriminatory action.

The Americans see black men and white women on the street in this country every day – and I have seen white Americans and coloured women together. Yet I have only heard of three incidents where there has been any trouble, and only in one case has there been fisticuffs. On that occasion the American soldier was sentenced to two years' imprisonment and was dishonourably discharged.

An American officer told me a few days ago that instructions are given each month to both white and coloured troops to 'mind their own business' and avoid racial conflicts. It is true he confessed that nothing was being done to cement relations between them but they were given strict orders 'about starting trouble' and the punishment was very severe if they did.

One solution to all the difficulty is obviously the appointment of West Indian liaison and welfare officers to these troops. There are about a dozen West Indian airmen who have completed their operational duties and are now instructors and given appointments as liaison officers to instructors. Could they not be given appointments as liaison officers to their newly arrived countrymen? It would be an inspiration to these recruits to meet their own West Indian friends who have been through the mill, who can share their confidences and help them in every way possible. I hope the Air Ministry and Colonial Office will consider this suggestion.

[*John Carter (General and Travelling Secretary), Newsletter, No. 63 (December 1944), pp. 59–60*]

Two of our members, members of the RAF, were assaulted at one of their weekly dances by two USA soldiers. When the matter was reported to their CO he gave them two bicycles with which to ride out into the country and advised them not to attend their weekly dances. They complied with this request but as one of them said in a letter, by doing so I am 'forfeiting my rights as a British subject and a member of the RAF.'

[*Newsletter, No. 63 (December 1944), p. 63*]

Dr Harold Moody wrote:

Some of our readers would like to have news of the Moody family: Captain Christine Moody, R.A.M.C., is a Staff Surgeon in the India Command and is now engaged to Captain Pat McDonough. They hope to be married in India in the Spring. Lieutenant H.E.A. Moody, R.A.M.C., is also in India. He was stationed 300 miles from his sister and was given three days' leave to go and see her. Captain Arundel Moody, R.W.K., has now been posted as Senior Captain to the 1st Caribbean Regiment, and is in the Middle East. This regiment is Britain's secret weapon, so secret she does not know of its existence. L.A.C. Ronald Moody has been in Italy for some time and has travelled about much. He was recently in a plane with Prince Umberto on the way to Rome. I learn with regret that Ronald is in hospital in Naples with a broken leg. A.C.2 Garth Moody is training somewhere in England.

[*Newsletter, No. 65 (February 1945), p. 103*]

FURTHER READING

Adams Earley, Charity, *One Woman's Army: A Black Officer Remembers the WAC* (Texas A & M University Press, 1989)

Adi, Hakim, *The History of the African and Caribbean Communities in Britain* (Wayland, 1995)

———, *West Africans in Britain 1900–1960: Nationalism, Pan-Africanism and Communism* (Lawrence and Wishart, 1998)

Adi, Hakim & Sherwood, Marika, *The 1945 Manchester Pan-African Congress Revisited* (New Beacon Books, 1995)

Anim-Addo, Joan, *Longest Journey: A History of Black Lewisham* (Deptford Forum Publishing, 1995)

Bader, Lilian, *Together: Lilian Bader: Wartime Memoirs of a WAAF 1939–1944* (Imperial War Museum, 1989)

Bourne, Stephen, 'We Also Served', *Black and Asian Studies Association Newsletter*, No. 35, January 2003, pp. 12–15

———, *Speak of Me As I Am: The Black Presence in Southwark Since 1600* (Southwark Council, 2005)

———, *Dr Harold Moody* (Southwark Council, 2008)

———, *Mother Country: Britain's Black Community on the Home Front, 1939–45* (The History Press, 2010)

Bourne, Stephen & Kyriacou, Sav (eds), *A Ship and a Prayer: The Black Presence in Hammersmith and Fulham* (ECOHP, 1999)

Bousquet, Ben & Douglas, Colin, *West Indian Women at War: British Racism in World War II* (Lawrence and Wishart, 1991)

Buggins, Joanne, 'West Indians in Britain during the Second World War: a short history drawing on Colonial Office papers', *Imperial War Museum Review No. 5* (Imperial War Museum, 1990)

Calder, Angus, *The People's War* (Jonathan Cape, 1969)

Clarke, Austin, *Growing Up Stupid Under the Union Jack: A Memoir* (Ian Randle, 2003)

Clarke, Peter B., *West Africans at War 1918–1914 and 1939–1945* (Ethnographica, 1986)

Constantine, Learie, *Colour Bar* (Stanley Paul, 1954)

Dabydeen, David, Gilmore, John & Jones, Cecily (eds), *The Oxford Companion to Black British History* (Oxford University Press, 2007)

Ethnic Communities Oral History Project, *The Motherland Calls: African Caribbean Experiences* (Hammersmith and Fulham Community History Series, No. 4/ECOHP, 1989)

Fadoyebo, Issac, *A Stroke of Unbelievable Luck* (African Studies Program/University of Wisconsin-Madison, 1999)

File, Nigel & Power, Chris, *Black Settlers in Britain 1555–1958* (Heinemann, 1981)

Ford, Amos A., *Telling the Truth: The Life and Times of the British Honduran Forestry Unit in Scotland (1941–44)* (Karia Press, 1985)

Francis, Martin, *The Flyer: British Culture and the Royal Air Force 1939–1945* (Oxford University Press, 2008)

Fryer, Peter, *Staying Power: The History of Black People in Britain* (Pluto, 1984)

Gardiner, Juliet, *Wartime Britain 1939–1945* (Headline, 2004)

Gilroy, Paul, *Black Britain: A Photographic History* (Saqi/Getty Images, 2007)

Grant, Cy, *'A Member of the RAF of Indeterminate Race': WW2 experiences of a former RAF Navigator and POW* (Woodfield Publishing, 2006)

———, *Blackness and the Dreaming Soul* (Shoving Leopard, 2007)

Haining, Peter, *The Day War Broke Out: 3 September 1939* (W.H. Allen, 1989)

Harriott, Jacqueline, *Black Women in Britain* (*Women Making History* series) (B.T. Batsford, 1992)

Heaton, Louis, 'For King and Country', *The Voice*, 12 November 1983, pp. 16–17

Henfrey, June & Law, Ian, *A History of Race and Racism in Liverpool, 1660–1950* (Merseyside Community Relations Council, 1981)

Howat, Gerald, *Learie Constantine* (George Allen, 1975)

Humphries, Steve, *The Call of the Sea: Britain's Maritime Past 1900–1960* (BBC Books, 1997)

Imperial War Museum, 'Together': a multimedia resource pack on the contribution made in the Second World War by African, Asian and Caribbean men and women (1995)

Jarrett-Macauley, Delia, *The Life of Una Marson 1905–65* (Manchester University Press, 1998)

Kakembo, Robert, *An African Soldier Speaks* (Edinburgh House Press, 1946)

Killingray, Professor David, 'African voices from two world wars', *Historical Research*, Vol. 74, No. 186, November 2000, pp 425–43.

———, *Fighting for Britain: African Soldiers in the Second World War* (James Currey, 2010)

Killingray, Professor David & Rathbone, Richard, *Africa and the Second World War* (Macmillan, 1986)

King, Sam, *Climbing Up the Rough Side of the Mountain* (Minerva Press, 1998)

Lambo, Roger, 'Achtung! The Black Prince: West Africans in the Royal Air Force 1939–46', in Professor David Killingray (ed.), *Africans in Britain* (Frank Cass, 1994)

Levy, Andrea, *Small Island* (Review, 2004)

Little, Kenneth, *Negroes in Britain: A Study in Racial Relations in English Society* (Kegan Paul, 1948)

Lotz, Rainer & Pegg, Ian, *Under the Imperial Carpet: Essays in Black History 1780–1950* (Rabbit Press, 1986)

Lusane, Clarence, *Hitler's Black Victims: The Historical Experiences of Afro-Germans, European Blacks, Africans, and African Americans in the Nazi Era* (Routledge, 2002)

McGuire, Phillip (ed.), *Taps for a Jim Crow Army: Letters from Black Soldiers in World War II* (University Press of Kentucky, 1983)

Marshall, Oliver, *The Caribbean at War: British West Indians in World War II* (North Kensington Archive, 1992)

Mason, Peter, *Caribbean Lives: Learie Constantine* (Signal Books, 2008)

Ministry of Defence, *We Were There* (2002)

Moore, Brenda L., *To Serve My Country, To Serve My Race: The Story of the Only African American WACs Stationed Overseas During World War II* (New York University Press, 1996)

Murray, Robert N., *Lest We Forget: The Experiences of World War II West Indian Ex-Service Personnel* (Nottingham West Indian Combined Ex-Services Association/Hansib, 1996)

Myers-Davis, Erica, *Under One Flag: How indigenous and ethnic peoples of the Commonwealth and British Empire helped Great Britain win World War II* (Get Publishing, 2009)

Noble, E. Martin, *Jamaica Airman: A Black Airman in Britain 1943 and After* (New Beacon Books, 1984)

Notting Dale Urban Studies Centre and Ethnic Communities Oral History Project, *Sorry No Vacancies: Life Stories of Senior Citizens from the Caribbean* (Notting Dale Urban Studies Centre/ECOHP, 1992)

Nunneley, John, *Tales from the King's African Rifles* (Cassell, 1998)

Osborne, Angelina & Torrington, Arthur, *We Served: The Untold Story of the West Indian Contribution to World War II* (Krik Krak Publishing, 2005)

Penick Motley, Mary, *The Invisible Soldier: The Experience of the Black Soldier, World War II* (Wayne State University Press, 1987)

Phillips, Mike & Phillips, Trevor, *Windrush: The Irresistible Rise of Multi-Racial Britain* (HarperCollins, 1998)

Reynolds, David, *Rich Relations: The American Occupation of Britain, 1942–1945* (HarperCollins, 1995)

Sandhu, Sukhdev, *London Calling: How Black and Asian Writers Imagined a City* (HarperCollins, 2003)

Schwarz, Bill (ed.), *West Indian Intellectuals in Britain* (Manchester University Press, 2003)

Scobie, Edward, *Black Britannia: A History of Blacks in Britain* (Johnson Publishing Company, 1972)

Sherwood, Marika, *Many Struggles: West Indian Workers and Service Personnel in Britain (1939–1945)* (Karia Press, 1985)

———, *Pastor Daniels Ekarte and the African Churches Mission* (The Savannah Press, 1994)

Sherwood, Marika & Spafford, Martin, *Whose Freedom Were Africans, Caribbeans and Indians Fighting for in World War II?* (The Savannah Press/Black and Asian Studies Association (pack for schools), 1999)

Sinclair, Neil M.C., *The Tiger Bay Story* (Butetown History and Arts Project, 1993)

Smith, Graham, 'Jim Crow on the Home Front (1942–1945)', *New Community*, III/33, Winter 1980, pp. 17–28.

———, *When Jim Crow Met John Bull: Black American Soldiers in World War II Britain* (I.B. Tauris, 1987)

Somerville, Christopher, *Our War: How the British Commonwealth Fought the Second World War* (Weidenfeld and Nicolson, 1998)

Spencer, Ian, 'World War Two and the Making of Multi-Racial Britain', in Pat Kirkham & David Thoms (eds), *War Culture: Social Change and Changing Experience in World War Two* (Lawrence and Wishart, 1995)

Spry Rush, Anne, *Bonds of Empire: West Indians and Britishness from Victoria to Decolonisation* (Oxford University Press, 2011)

Thompson, Dudley, *From Kingston to Kenya: The Making of a Pan-Africanist Lawyer* (The Majority Press, 1993)

Thompson, Leslie & Green, Jeffrey, *Swing from a Small Island: Tkhe Story of Leslie Thompson* (Northway Publications, 2009)

Vaughan, David A., *Negro Victory: The Life Story of Dr Harold Moody* (Independent Press, 1950)

Walker, Sam & Elcock, Alvin (eds), *The Windrush Legacy: Memories of Britain's post-war Caribbean Immigrants* (The Black Cultural Archives, 1998)

Webster, Wendy, *Englishness and Empire 1939–1965* (Oxford University Press, 2005)

Weekes, Danielle, 'War of Words (60 years after D-Day, history must be rewritten to include tales of black servicemen)', *The Voice*, 31 May 2004, pp. 12–13

West, Peter, 'Rank Outsiders', *The Listener*, 8 November 1990, pp. 9–11

Wilson, Carlton, 'Liverpool's Black Population During World War II', *Black and Asian Studies Association Newsletter*, No. 20, January 1998, 6–18

Wynn, Neil A., '"Race War": Black American GIs and West Indians in Britain during the Second World War', *Immigrants and Minorities*, Vol. 24, No. 3, November 2006, 324–46

Ziegler, Philip, *London at War 1939–1945* (Sinclair-Stevenson, 1995)

ABOUT THE AUTHOR

Stephen Bourne brings great natural scholarship and passion to a largely hidden story. He is highly accessible, accurate, and surprising. You always walk away from his work knowing something that you didn't know, that you didn't even suspect.

Bonnie Greer, playwright and critic

Born in the London Borough of Southwark, Stephen was raised on a housing estate on Peckham Road and left school at the age of 16 with no qualifications. Self-taught, in 1983 he began writing for black British journals, including the newspaper *The Voice*.

STEPHEN BOURNE'S BLACK BRITISH HISTORY TIMELINE

1983   Programmed *Burning an Illusion* for the National Film Theatre, the first black British film retrospective

1985   Film consultant for the Greater London Council's 'Paul Robeson' exhibition at the Royal Festival Hall

1988   Graduated from the London College of Printing with a Bachelor of Arts Degree in Film and Television

1989–92 Employed by the British Film Institute/BBC as a researcher

1991   Co-authored his first book, *Aunt Esther's Story*, with his adopted aunt, Esther Bruce (1912–94), a black working-class Londoner; the book was published by Hammersmith and Fulham's Ethnic Communities Oral History Project (ECOHP)

1991   A founder member of the Black and Asian Studies Association with, among others, Sean Creighton, Marika Sherwood, Dr Hakim Adi, Peter Fryer, Jeffrey Green, Professor David Killingray and Howard Rye

1992   Co-researcher on *Black and White in Colour*, a two-part BBC television documentary directed by Isaac Julien – based on a ground-breaking project that unearthed the history of race and representation on British television

1992   Programmed the *Black and White in Colour* television retrospective for the National Film Theatre

1993   First Commission for Racial Equality *Race in the Media* award for BBC Radio 2's *Salutations* series (presented by Moira Stuart) that celebrated black British, African and Caribbean musicians and singers in Britain in the 1930s, 1940s and 1950s

1994   Second Commission for Racial Equality *Race in the Media* award for BBC Radio 2's *Black in the West End* (presented by Clarke Peters), a celebration of black musical theatre in London's West End

1996   Programmed *Black on White TV*, the National Film Theatre's second black British television retrospective which included tributes to actors Norman Beaton and Carmen Munroe

1996   Second edition of *Aunt Esther's Story* published by ECOHP

1998   Researched and scripted the BBC Radio 2 series *Their Long Voyage Home* (presented by Sir Trevor McDonald) for the BBC's *Windrush* season

1998   Programmed the National Film Theatre's film and television retrospective: *Song of Freedom: A Centenary Tribute to Paul Robeson*

1999   Began working as a voluntary independent adviser to the police in the London Borough of Southwark

2001   *Black in the British Frame: The Black Experience in British Film and Television*, published by Continuum for which he was nominated for *The Voice* Black Community Award for Literature and received a Civic Award from the London Borough of Southwark

2001   *Sophisticated Lady: A Celebration of Adelaide Hall*, published by ECOHP

2001   Presented the first of many illustrated talks about black participation in the Second World War at the Imperial War Museum, London

2002   Won the Metropolitan Police Volunteer Award for advice on critical incidents, including the murder of Peckham schoolboy Damilola Taylor

2004   Began contributing biographies about black Britons to the *Oxford Dictionary of National Biography* (Oxford University Press) and by 2012 Stephen's total had reached thirty-five

2005   *Elisabeth Welch: Soft Lights and Sweet Music*, published by Scarecrow Press

2005   *Speak of Me As I Am: The Black Presence in Southwark Since 1600*, published by Southwark Council

2006   Graduated from De Montfort University in Leicester with a Master of Philosophy degree

2007   Contributed to *The Oxford Companion to Black British History*, published by Oxford University Press

2008   Curated 'Keep Smiling Through: Black Londoners on the Home Front 1939–45', an exhibition for the Cuming Museum in the London Borough of Southwark

2008   Consultant on 'From War to Windrush', an exhibition for the Imperial War Museum, London

2008   *Dr Harold Moody*, published by Southwark Council

2010   *Mother Country: Britain's Black Community on the Home Front, 1939–45*, published by The History Press

2012   Third edition of *Aunt Esther's Story*, published, revised and retitled *Esther Bruce: A Black London Seamstress: Her Story 1912–1994* by History and Social Action Publications

For further information go to www.stephenbourne.co.uk

INDEX